# They Will Always Meet At Eleven

*Also by Jim Meads*
THEY STILL MEET AT ELEVEN

*The incomparable Lionel Edwards finishing his painting of the running photographer in action with the Belvoir.*

# They Will Always
# Meet At Eleven

JIM MEADS

With drawings by John King

Foreword by HRH The Prince of Wales

QUILLER PRESS
LONDON

To hunt servants, past and present, everywhere, without whose help my most difficult of jobs would have been almost impossible and far less enjoyable.

First published 1991 by Quiller Press Ltd
46 Lillie Road, London SW6 1TN

Text and illustrations copyright © Jim Meads 1991
Drawings © John King 1991

ISBN 0 870948 70 X

Produced by Hugh Tempest-Radford *Book Producers*
Typeset by Goodfellow & Egan Phototypesetting Limited
Printed in Great Britain by
St Edmundsbury Press

# Contents

# *Foreword*
# *by HRH The Prince of Wales*

Jim Meads is one of those remarkable characters who seems to have unbounded energy and enthusiasm. As far as I can make out he has succeeded in running over most of the hunting country in England, Scotland, Wales and Ireland, not to mention half the United States of America as well! His stamina is unbounded and his fitness for a man of his age is little short of superhuman. How he manages to take such good photographs after all his exertions is beyond my comprehension. I find it tiring enough on a horse!

I am sure this book will give great pleasure to all those, in all walks of life, who thrill at the sound of the hunting horn and at the cry of a hound.

# *Introduction*

I find it difficult to realise that I am now in my forty-second season as a field sports photographer. It seems only yesterday that, on arrival at the Bicester hunt kennels, I was greeted by Mrs Lloyd-Mostyn, the senior joint master, with the words: 'You haven't come to take pictures have you, you're much too young.' (At the time I was all of twenty-one and very hard up.) Having a father who was a photographer, until the War, on the staff of *Country Life*, I had never dreamed of doing anything but take photos when I grew up, unless it was to be a pilot in the Royal Air Force.

When I was six, I was taught to ride by the legendary Miss Joan Middleton, in Hertfordshire, becoming an early member of the Enfield Chace Pony Club, and in my first season's hunting I was blooded by Ted Cox, the huntsman, deep in Broxbourne Woods. Then came the war, when we survived not only the Battle of Britain but also the 'doodlebugs', one of which blew our house down on top of us on 1 July, 1944. Two years later, aged sixteen, I left Hertford Grammar School to become a trainee photographer at the De Havilland Aircraft Co., flying with such wartime heroes as 'Cat's Eyes' Cunningham and John Derry. However, on Saturdays I was running after our local packs of hounds with a camera, occasionally having a picture published. Then came National Service, a mostly enjoyable twenty months as an R.A.F lorry driver (so much for becoming a pilot).

In May 1950 came 'demob', from which date I became a full-time field sports photographer, gradually venturing further afield on my motor cycle, as I couldn't yet afford a car. By now foxhunting was recovering from the war and many of the famous 1930s huntsmen were still in office showing tremendous sport, as more and more people joined in. At this time my camera was an old Thornton Pickard, with no means of measuring focus or exposure, which was all a matter of guesswork. It was also pretty heavy as it took pictures on 5 × 4 inch glass plates, which are still in my files today. Gradually the fox hunting world came to recognise me and, with all my energetic footslogging, I became known as 'the running photographer'. Today, after countless thousands of cross-country miles under all conditions, I'm still convinced that mine is the only way to take proper hunting pictures. It is desperately hard work but so rewarding when you make a correct decision and reach the right place at the right time, to record a spectacular scene that could not be recorded in any other way.

In 1957, three of my ambitions were achieved: I acquired an Austin A30 van (62 mph flat out); my old camera was pensioned off and a fine modern MPP Press camera took its place, and for the first time one of my hunting pictures appeared on the cover of *Horse and Hound*. I reckoned I had arrived. Then two years later Sir Andrew Horsburgh-Porter was appointed hunting correspondent of *The Field* and he asked me to accompany him on his expeditions. We worked together with never a cross word until he retired in 1971 and it was Sir Andrew who introduced me to the delights of hunting in Ireland, during the terrible winter of 1962–3. I've enjoyed my visits to the Emerald Isle ever since.

The year 1973 marked another milestone in my career. One day I was out with the Old Surrey and Burstow, following a very wet meet from Horne Grange and taking pictures for Michael Clayton, with whom I had worked for some ten years. He turned to me at a dripping covert side and said, 'You're not going to believe this, but I'm to be the next editor of *Horse and Hound*.' Soon 'Foxford's' hunting diary became one of the most eagerly read sections of *Horse and Hound* and it has been my privilege to have taken the photos for almost every one of them, not only in the UK but also in America, where they thought I was a 'mad Brit' when I said that I would follow on foot.

Over the years I have watched many changes taking place, among them the ploughing of old turf and the grubbing out of hedgerows, and the tremendous increase in the number of people who follow hounds on horseback and in cars, sometimes to the detriment of a straight hunt. Today, in almost every country, there are commercial pheasant shoots where foxes are controlled by hard-pressed keepers, while the latest phenomenon is an explosion in the number of golf courses. But one change which has helped the fox, hounds and the running photographer – although not the mounted field – is the increase in winter corn. It is possible to run over it almost as well as grass, unlike the deep and heavy plough of bygone years.

To date I have photographed 397 different packs of hounds and, while I don't have an outright favourite, my home pack for the past six seasons – the David Davies – in its splendid wild and mountainous country of mid Wales, is near the top. Of course I love too the heady atmosphere of High Leicestershire where, although I know I will have the most strenuous day's work, it is worth every drop of sweat just to witness the cut and thrust of the riders. Equally I enjoy a day with a small pack where the committee keep things going on a shoestring budget with a single-handed huntsman. For me, a day with beagles is relaxing because it is all about hound work, as indeed is a visit to the Lake District, although on occasions, when endeavouring to climb a particularly steep and rocky mountain, with lungs about to burst, I wonder why on earth I do it; but not for long as the feeling of exhilaration on reaching the summit makes all the pain worth while.

Although I have now completed forty-one seasons I still have ambitions: to finish photographing all the foxhunts in the UK, to pass the 400-hunts barrier and to stay fit enough to carry on running for many more years, even though I reached my sixtieth birthday on 9 July 1990. On that day I was fortunate enough to lunch at Highgrove House with HRH The Prince of Wales, whose presence in the hunting field over the past sixteen seasons has given so much pleasure to so many people. Things certainly have changed for me since 1950.

*Mr Bill Read MFH with the Amwell Valley hounds at the end of a day in New Jersey.*

*Joint master Mr Gordon Smith with a squashed hat after his girth broke.*

# The Amwell Valley, New Jersey, USA

'We meet at 8.30 a.m. on Sunday, at Oliver Toigo's farm near Ringoes in Hunterdon County,' said Mr Bill Read, joint master and huntsman of the Amwell Valley Foxhounds in New Jersey, founded in 1960. I had first met Bill Read when he was enjoying a day with the Warwickshire during a winter holiday in England, and there and then he invited me to come and visit the Amwell Valley. Joint master Mr Dick Hudnut is also field master and he had his work cut out on the day of my visit in November 1977 for, with sixty mounted followers, it was one of the biggest turnouts in the history of the hunt. When I arrived, half an hour early, there were already numerous trailers parked, their occupants ready for the off.

The Amwell country is intensively farmed – even the headlands are ploughed in – and a tremendous amount of fertiliser is applied, so scenting conditions are usually poor. The grass was crisp and white after a hard overnight frost, but the sun was coming up and conditions soon improved. The ten couple of cross-bred hounds, many by Essex (USA) stallions out of Heythrop bitches, hit off a cold drag on Mr Manners's farm, which they hunted patiently through maize, soy beans, woods and stubble until stopped by a field of semi-frozen plough. A good red fox was then found in soy beans and, taking to the grass, hounds began to fly and the riders had to kick on to keep in touch. Coops and timber sped beneath the horses' hooves as they galloped across Knobby Knoll Farm where hounds checked in uncut maize. A good cast had them running on again over the grass of Wilenta's Farm and across the main road to ground in a bank above the creek after a useful forty-five minutes. Another exciting chase promised as the pack put up a fox in gorse on Pine Twig Farm. Getting away on good terms, hounds ran hard across stubble and grass, into uncut maize again where this fox took a wrong turn and was caught. Then it was back to the meet for an enormous hunt breakfast, which the happy hunt followers despatched with equal gusto.

I

*Mr Martin Salter MH with hounds as they hit off the line of their fox, after a check.*

# The Axe Vale Harriers, Devon

What could be more down-to-earth than a pack of hounds run by a farmers' committee, with farmers as huntsman and whippers-in and followed mainly by farmers and their families? Such is the case in South Devon where the Axe Vale Harriers hunt the fox, although their white West Country harriers are still registered in the Harrier Stud Book. The much-respected Len Newbury was acting master and huntsman 1949–68; then Major Peter Wainwright held this office for three seasons, when he was succeeded by Martin Salter who had been a whipper-in since 1949 and whose grandfather was a member of the original committee which formed the pack in 1885. Today Martin is going as well as ever and was honoured in 1989 by being elected president of the Masters of Harriers and Beagles Association.

On this particular day in November 1977 hounds met at Southleigh, in weather which was too sunny and mild for November, and a busy day was spent in idyllic Devonshire countryside, with its steeply sloping grass fields and rough combes, hairy banks and colourful woods and gorse coverts. West-Country harriers, being mostly white, are easier to see than their brown relations, a blessing when the first fox was marked to ground in a veritable jungle of rhododendrons. He was left, then hounds hit off a drag in Whitmore Gorse and worked up to their second fox which led them a merry dance up and down those steep valleys and out onto the heather-clad moorland of Warren Hill. Scent in the sunshine was moderate and this eighty-five-minute hunt petered out amongst the thick gorses on Wilcombe Common, but by early afternoon the sun had gone, the air turned cold and scent improved dramatically! Finding in Bull Hall Gorse, the pack were soon into top gear, tremendous hound music echoed along the combes and the fox broke into the open on Warren Hill. But the pace was too hot and, turning down into Whitmore Gorse, he was caught after a thrilling twenty-five minutes gallop, mostly on old turf.

3

*Mr Brian Cornelius MFH leading the field through the yards of a colliery.*

*The end of a good hunt.*

# *The Banwen Miners,*
# *West Glamorgan*

The 'people's pack', the Banwen Miners, in the Welsh Valleys of West Glamorgan, was formed amidst a clamour of publicity twenty-nine years ago. Initially it was an all-amateur set-up from the village of Banwen with joint masters Tom Jones and Tom Hopkins (who remained in office until 1976), and with hounds kennelled in the old lamp room at the now-disused local coal-mine. Gradually the hunt widened its horizons, joint masters came in from Swansea, and in 1975 John Davies became the first professional huntsman.

The Banwen country is varied, with forestry and steep rough valleys; an area of well-fenced grassy vale, and stretches of rolling moorland and stone walls, which hasn't changed for many years. I visited there in January 1979 during one of the 'big freezes' which we used to suffer but, with the meet being close to the 'warmer' sea, it was one of the few hunts not stopped by frost and snow. George Watkins was huntsman and Brian Cornelius the master in charge at a very convivial meet held at the local hostelry. Always ready for a bit of a lark, the mounted field of eighty had to clear a show-jump fence on the way to the first draw, 'just to warm the blood on this perishing morning!' A fox was soon found in a thick valley and caught after a twisty run. Another was then accounted for and the pack moved on towards more open country, leaving me on the wrong side of the river. As I ran on I could see that the field would have to pass through a colliery, making this a picture not to be missed, so I quickly waded the icy river (luckily only waist deep), with the result you see here. Later there was a four-mile hunt across marvellous old moorland turf, a joy to gallop over. Hounds finally marked their fox to ground on a snow-covered slope overlooking Ammanford. I *had* to run fast because I was so cold and wet around my nether regions – so much so that I arrived at the earth before many of the horses.

*Mr Michael Milburn MH taking hounds to draw from Hagley Bridge Farm.*

# *The Beacon Beagles,*
# *Somerset*

The Beacon Beagles whose country is in west Somerset and Devon, were bravely started in 1940, when the Battle of Britain was raging, by Michael Roffe-Silvester. His brother Peter joined him in 1942 and it remained a family pack until 1958. Two years later hounds were bought by Mr and Mrs T. Jones, but folded after five seasons; they were re-formed in 1966, only to disband again three years later. In 1970 the present Beacon Beagles were started by Michael Milburn, who was joined in control after ten seasons by John Price and Roly Milton, and they have gone from strength to strength. They have even managed to breed hounds back to the 'old Beacon' through Kinsman '64, thus re-forging a link with the Roffe-Silvesters who now run their own pack of foxhounds from the same kennels at Reaphay, West Buckland.

In December 1983 I joined a splendid meet at Hagley Bridge Farm and as we moved off along a typical narrow winding Somerset lane to draw a large cone-shaped hill, the regulars told me that I had come on the right day as all I had to do was stand on top of the hill and watch the hares being hunted round and round! I was not convinced and, as always, kept my options open. Initially it seemed that the 'hilltoppers' were correct as the hares *did* run in circles. Then, after one short check, Kevin Price viewed our hare away down the hill. 'She'll soon be back,' murmured the knowledgeable ones, but I wasn't so sure as hounds were really motoring. Taking the plunge, I loped down to the valley bottom and across the stream as hounds in full cry climbed out on the far side. On and on the energetic few ran, by now out of sight and sound of the pack. By Ashbrittle village we met them as they returned from Stanley via the river Tone. After fresh-finding this brave hare, hounds raced away again to circle the village, finally being stopped at dusk after a great hunt, with a three mile point which only eight of us ran to the finish. The remainder were still on their hilltop awaiting the pack's return.

7

*HRH The Prince of Wales and Belvoir huntsman Robin Jackson with hounds near Scalford.*

*Mr John Blakeway MFH, leading the way from Hose Thorns in a fierce hailstorm.*

## The Belvoir, Lincolnshire & Leicestershire

The Belvoir, one of England's most historic hunts, was formed in 1750. Over the years I have spent many happy days with the Duke of Rutland's famous 'Old English' foxhounds, where the doghounds hunt the ploughlands of Lincolnshire and the bitches do their duty on the more fashionable grass of Leicestershire. Amongst the many Belvoir masters during these years the longest-serving has been Mr John King, whom I first met in 1955 when he was master of the Badsworth Hunt in Yorkshire; now, as Lord King of British Airways fame, he is hunt chairman. It has also been my privilege to know three long-serving huntsmen and to photograph each of them in action: in November 1955 I went to Croxton Park to see George Tongue (1928–56) carrying the horn at his last opening meet, when 'young' Jim Webster was his whipper-in; Jim then took over and hunted hounds in his individual and successful way until 1983, when Robin Jackson assumed control. I returned to Croxton Park for the new huntsman's first opening meet on a brilliantly sunny day.

In recent years, the size of the mounted field has been limited, but in days gone by there seemed to be around 300 horses on parade, and what a spectacle they made as they galloped across those undulating grasslands of High Leicestershire. And what a buzz of excitement fills the air as hounds race away from Clawson Thorns and those most thrusting of riders tackle the downhill fences with much splintering of wood and emptying of saddles, skirting Clawson village and heading into the vale beyond. Then at Hose Thorns there is always an expectant hush as the field master holds everyone back until the fox leaves covert (usually in the right direction); then his hand drops and the cavalry charge begins towards the delectable line of thorn hedges crossing the vale towards Sherbrookes, from where so many good hunts have begun.

*Tim Langley with hounds on the banks of the river Severn.*

*Berkeley whipper-in Patrick Martin with a bitch and whelps.*

---

# The Berkeley, Gloucestershire

Even the name, the Earl of Berkeley's Foxhounds, has a historical ring to it; and so it should for the hunt dates from 1613 and has its kennels close to Berkeley Castle, completed in 1153 and the home of the Berkeley family ever since. In its early days the hunt's country extended as far as London and the famous yellow livery worn by hunt staff and male masters is also worn by the Vale of Aylesbury Hunt, which encompasses the former Old Berkeley Hunt country. The present occupant of the castle is Major John Berkeley, who owns the pack and was joint master from 1960 until 1984. Sadly, it is a tradition there not to show hounds, which is a great pity as they have some splendid examples of the modern foxhound; indeed, such stallions as David '81, Fencer '84, Freshman '84 and Gambler '85 are in widespread demand and sire many excellent progeny.

The Berkeley country is still much laid to grass, the fields often being divided by enormous ditches called rhines into which horse and rider can and do disappear, emerging wet and smelly! Several meets are held close to the river Severn and it was at one of these in October 1980, at the Berkeley Arms, Purton, close to the Slimbridge Wildfowl Trust, that I took this picture of the much-loved Tim Langley. He was in charge of the kennels from 1951 to 1981, carrying the horn for the last fourteen of those glorious years and showing tremendous sport throughout. On this day, although it was an 8 a.m. cub-hunting meet, a big field assembled and they were not disappointed. Foxes were found everywhere, including on the banks of the Sharpness Canal and one was caught actually on the railway lines at Sharpness docks. By 1.30 p.m. we were in the Deer Park, close to home, and hounds caught a fifth fox to end a long and successful morning in warm sunshine.

# The Bermingham and North Galway, Ireland

One of the many attractions of hunting is the element of danger inherent to riding a horse across country at speed. In a normal day out one meets run-of-the-mill hedges, timber, walls or ditches, but on an odd occasion a really horrendous obstacle rears up and, if jumped successfully, is remembered for ever. Of all the 'frighteners' I have seen during forty years in the hunting field, this one remains in my memory most vividly. I was in Ireland with Major Mike MacEwan, reporting on the Bermingham and North Galway Hunt, founded in 1946. We had been invited to stay with the senior lady joint master who guided us to the meet at Shrule, in sight of the coast (that is, when the view wasn't blotted out by one of the frequent, bitterly cold blizzards being blown in from the Atlantic). On this day, in January 1983, huntsman Henry Gordon and his hounds kept things moving, then late in the afternoon the pack really began to run hard. Determined to keep in touch, a few brave souls jumped this fearsome place, a bridge without any parapets, across which a wall had been built to keep cattle in. On each side was a twenty-foot drop into a river yet this picture shows how cleanly Major MacEwan cleared it to win the hunt.

Next morning, as we were saying good-bye to our hostess – well known for being a bit of a character, she said, 'Before you go I want you to do something for me.' Expecting to be asked to sign the visitors' book, we were both left speechless when this good lady presented us each with a bill and said, 'Please pay now!'

*No room for error! Major Mike MacEwan clearing the frightening bridge described above.*

# The Blencathra, Cumbria

The life of fell huntsmen is desperately hard and one which, apart from the arrival of the Land Rover and the hound trailer, has changed little during the past century. Amongst this breed of hardy individuals, the late Johnny Richardson of the Blencathra is remembered with special affection by many thousands of locals and visitors alike who have come to the Lake District to hunt with the legendary John Peel's hounds since the foundation of the pack as far back as records go. Johnny Richardson was born in 1919 and was a shepherd until the last war when he enlisted, seeing much active service before being captured at Tobruk in North Africa. He escaped three times, and finally succeeded, after walking hundreds of miles through the Apennines, in rejoining the British forces. In 1946 he became whipper-in to George Bell at the Blencathra and three years later was appointed huntsman, a post he filled with distinction until his death at the kennels in 1988.

From small beginnings in 1949, Johnny bred an excellent pack of fox-catching hounds, initially with blood lines from the Border, the College Valley and the Plas Machynlleth. Now his stallion hounds are used, not only in the fells, but also in lowland packs and in America. My picture shows Johnny, with Barry Todhunter, who now carries the horn, leading hounds from the opening meet at Threlkeld into his beloved mountainous and rocky country where I'm sure his spirit roams today, as free as the winds which howl around the Cumbrian crags he hunted so well.

*The Blencathra's Johnny Richardson and Barry Todhunter taking hounds to draw above Threlkeld.*

Michael Hedley MFH with his hounds on the hills near Hindhope.

Many shepherds follow hounds on motor-bikes or ATVs.

# *The Border,*
# *Northumberland*

This is the picture which Michael Hedley's friends rather unkindly said that I would never be able to take, as it shows him with eight couple of hounds during a day's hunting! What they really meant was that the Border Foxhounds range so far and wide whilst drawing that there are never any working close to him! Michael has been joint master and huntsman since 1973 when he joined his father Ian, who has been in office since 1954. With the pack kennelled at the Hedley's Overacres Farm in Otterburn, the Border's family tradition continues for, since 1869, only members of the Robson, Dobb and Hedley families have been masters and eligible to wear those famous steel-grey coats.

You need to be hardy to hunt with the Border because the weather is often bitterly cold and wet, yet it is part of the way of life in this predominantly sheep-farming area.

In 1903 the country was described as almost all moorland, with a little plough and no woodland. Now there are vast tracts of forestry which make hunting difficult, although they do provide a haven for foxes – which they certainly need because the Border hounds are among the most efficient fox-catchers anywhere. Unlike many packs, these hill hounds expect to catch every fox they find and it is not uncommon for them to have a run of twenty miles or more across their beautiful hill country before bringing the hunt to a successful finish. Amazingly enough, where the normal procedure during the summer is for the pack to be walked out or exercised with bicycles or ponies for a couple of hours a day, the Border are rumoured to stay in kennels right through the summer. However, many masters are immensely impressed by them, and use their stallion hounds. It was Border blood which Sir Alfred Goodson turned to when starting the College Valley Hunt in 1924 and today they are still using it. Long may the Hedleys and their fiercely loyal supporters carry on the good work.

*Action in the river Severn on a hot summer's day near Caersws, Montgomeryshire.*

# The Border Counties Minkhounds, Montgomeryshire

During the late 1960's and through to the end of 1977, I spent many marvellous summer days hunting in Wales and the borders with Ray and Jackie Williams, masters of the Border Counties Otterhounds. They were tremendous times when the weather always seemed good and bright sunshine warmed the water, for those mountain rivers can be cold. Ray and Jackie had a fine team to support them: the ever-friendly Harry Kendrick was the first whipper-in and he was joined by followers from as far away as Birmingham who made the long journey to the peace and tranquillity of Wales, to hunt the otter and enjoy glorious days in spectacular scenery. John Bridge, then the honorary secretary, later became a joint master and deputy huntsman whilst Ian Coghill was in charge of the hunt supporters club; now he does so much to defend hunting as a public relations officer for the British Field Sports Society.

One of my most memorable hunts came on 29 June 1974, on the river Severn, from a meet at the Red Lion in Llandinam, close by the David Davies Foxhounds kennels. After a most exciting three-and-three-quarter hours, much of it spent in deep water, a big dog otter was caught, and I have one of his pads on my office wall as a trophy of this chase. Four years later the otter was made a protected animal and most of the packs, and many newly formed ones, emerged to hunt mink, which have spread like wildfire throughout most of the United Kingdom. Ferocious killers, mink are decimating fish, water fowl and anything else living within reach of the river, and in July 1987 I again spent a day on the Severn, close to Caersws, to see the mink hounds, hunted by John Newton, tackle the local population. Three were caught and then, later on, one left the water and was marked under a car and disappeared. Eventually the car bonnet was raised and the mink bolted, to be added to the tally – strange but true!

Long-serving Brandywine huntsman John White collecting his
American hounds at the end of a
day in Pennsylvania.

Mrs Jane Sullivan MFH, who
has been master since 1959.

# The Brandywine, Pennsylvania, USA

One of the longer-established packs of foxhounds in America, the Brandy-wine was formed in 1892 by Mr Charles Mather who, strange though it may sound, had drafts from the Belvoir. In 1928 his son Gilbert took over and changed to the lower-scenting American hounds which they continue to breed and hunt today. It is, however, still very much a family pack – indeed a private one – for in 1959 Mrs Jane Sullivan succeeded her father in the mastership and was joined in 1987 by her daughter, Lindy Bedwell, who had whipped-in for much of her life. Professional huntsman John White has also spent a lifetime with the Brandywine, having been at the kennels in Chester County, Pennysylvania since the war. Continuing the family theme again, John has his daughter Brenda as field master.

The meet I joined was held at Mr Baldwin's farm on a dry, bright morning in November 1980 following a hard overnight frost and twenty-six-and-a-half couple of tri-coloured American hounds were produced by hunt staff immaculately turned out in their wine-coloured livery. Close on fifty mounted followers arrived in time to see the pack find their first fox and leave covert with a tremendous cry. The ground was exceptionally dry and at times dusty; however, much of the country is beautiful rolling grassland, with areas of light arable and more than enough cover to hold a good population of foxes whilst the rough valleys teem with deer, which hounds totally ignore. During the day we crossed the Brandywine river and marked three foxes to ground after useful and musical hunts.

Then, as a bonus, Mrs Sullivan and John White took me back to the kennels for a conducted tour and a super hunt 'breakfast', which went down well after my energetic day's running.

*Mrs Betty Gingell, master and huntsman of the Cambridgeshire Harriers since 1942, showing how to cross the country.*

## The Cambridgeshire Harriers

'From one extreme to the other' is an accurate appraisal of the history of the Cambridgeshire Harriers. Founded in 1745, when roads were few and far between, they were originally a farmers' pack. Then, being close to Cambridge, university students became involved in the mastership so there were many inevitable changes in control. Two of the more recent undergraduate masters are now familiar names in foxhunting: Mr Richard Barlow (1934–6) was MFH at Chiddingfold, Leconfield and Cowdray 1936–90, and Major Richard Dill (1940–1) was a joint master of the Warwickshire. However, in 1942 a most significant change occurred which transformed the fortunes of the hunt: Mrs Betty Gingell became master and huntsman, kennelling hounds at her home Horningsea Manor from where she and her husband Hugh farm extensively. Today she is still master and, even more amazingly is still hunting hounds on the top-class heavyweight hunters required to jump the numerous ditches which abound in the area. Her hounds too are outstanding year after year winning championships at Peterborough, where it is jokingly said that the only way to stop Mrs Gingell from winning is to make her the judge! She has taken many hunter championships over the years and exported hounds to countries as far away as New Zealand. Her hounds hunt as well as they look on the flags and each season catch a good tally of hares on their heavy plough country – and even a fox or two – so they have plenty of pace and stamina. Betty Gingell's reign has been a famous one and I'm looking forward to joining in the celebrations to commemorate her next milepost as master and huntsman.

Johnnie O'Shea, the Cheshire's huntsman 1966–91, taking hounds to a fresh draw.

Hunt chairman Mr John Boddington in action.

# The Cheshire

When it was announced that Johnnie O'Shea, the Cheshire huntsman since 1966, was to retire on 1 May 1991 an air of great sadness suffused the hunt's country. It is not too much of an exaggeration to say that, for those twenty-five years, Johnnie had kept the Cheshire at the top of the tree, through numerous changes of mastership, with his good humour and ability with hounds and people. If ever a man was destined to be a huntsman it was Johnnie. Born at the Queen's County kennels, where his father was a long-time whipper-in, he reached the Cheshire via the Wexford, Warwickshire and Meynell and here set about breeding a pack of hounds which mirrored his personality: fast and musical (Johnnie, after all, did win the *Horse and Hound* horn-blowing championship in 1990) a joy to the eye, great fox-catchers and fun to hunt with, even on the less good days. The Cheshire hounds' good looks have won them numerous championships at the summer shows, where Johnnie is a master showman.

The Cheshire was founded in 1763. Its country is still basically grass with numerous dairy farms although, sadly, some of the best of the old turf and the challenging fences around Saighton with its notorious brook, in which many a brave thruster has been totally immersed, is now a prairie of winter corn. Amongst many memorable days I've spent with Johnnie, this picture was taken on one of the best, from a meet held at Cholmondeley Castle in February 1979 during a spell of hard frost. The first fox ran across the ice on the lake, which was worrying as hounds followed, but happily without disaster. At the end of the day only six riders out of a field of 130 – including a somewhat muddied Prince of Wales – were still in attendance, so fast and furious had been the pace.

Johnnie O'Shea's ebullient wit will be greatly missed by his fellow professionals. It is a racing certainty that, no matter who comes to hunt the Cheshire country in the future, things will never be quite the same without his genius and wonderful Irish blarney.

The Cottesmore hounds in full cry, away from a leafy Lady-wood, after an early opening meet.

Capt Brian Fanshawe MFH, away from Ladywood.

# The Cottesmore, Leicestershire

One of the world-famous 'Melton hunts', the Cottesmore is different to its neighbours of High Leicestershire in that invariably hounds have been hunted by a joint master rather than a professional huntsman. Over the years since its formation in 1666, such well-known characters as Major Chetty Hilton-Green, Lt Col Cyril Heber Percy, Lt Col Sir Henry Tate, Major Robert Hoare and Captain Simon Clarke have all carried the horn, whilst the present incumbent, Captain Brian Fanshawe, is as full-bloodied a fox-catcher as you'll find anywhere. Apart from being a great hound man, Captain Fanshawe is also brilliant across country and has won many races under National Hunt rules and in point-to-points.

In recent years the weather patterns of England have changed tremendously and the traditional opening meet now seems to take place in October, instead of the first Saturday in November. Even so, I suspect that this picture of hounds flying away from Ladywood, following the opening meet at Preston Lodge on 18 October 1983, remains amongst the earliest, as you can see from the lush foliage on the trees. Bright sunshine glinted on the mounted field that day whilst the riders, turned out in their best, tried to look nonchalant despite the inevitable butterflies in the stomach at the thought of the big fences to be jumped on hard autumnal ground. For once, as hounds drew Ladywood, I guessed right, and was perfectly placed to see the fox leave and to photograph hounds in full cry as they raced uphill towards Orton Park and Wilson's Gorse. Hard on their heels came the field of thrusters headed by field master Mr Joss Hanbury and I managed to take some equally splendid action pictures of horse and rider jumping fences in perfect harmony.

*Huntsman Cliff Standing with his hounds after catching their fox at the end of a seventy-minute hunt.*

# *The Crawley and Horsham, West Sussex*

I find it quite extraordinary that, despite being so close to London, parts of the Crawley and Horsham country, hunted over so keenly by their followers since 1840, are quite isolated and wild. Although without many natural fences, the whole area is admirably served by hunt jumps and tiger traps so that it is possible to stay in touch with hounds without having to use the roads too much. Also, where there is arable land, wide headlands have been left unploughed to ensure that the hunt is not unduly delayed by having to creep around the corn in single file.

The old adage about not going home early from hunting because often the best hunts come late in the day was well and truly brought home to the followers after this meet at Thakeham Place in February 1987. Overnight frost had given way to a bright day, but there was a bitterly cold wind and initially scent seemed poor. However, huntsman Cliff Standing and his hounds kept the large mounted field busy.

Nonetheless, many people had gone home when Cliff said, 'I'll just draw those big round bales at Dick Sawyer's on the way back.' As if on cue, no less than two brace of foxes bolted and hounds were laid on the line of the right one, which proceeded to lead them a merry dance across the Sussex countryside. Several times the huntsman made good casts, especially when the A24 dual carriageway intervened, but after a grand seventy-minute hound hunt covering some nine miles, the fox was killed at 5.05 p.m. when there was just enough light left for me to take this picture of the end.

29

*A timeless picture of the Culm-
stock hunt staff in 1973, showing
David Allibone, Charlie Mott,
Norman Bartlett MH and
Anthony Allibone with hounds at
Reaphay.*

*Master and huntsman Mr Nor-
man Bartlett with hounds in the
river Exe.*

# The Culmstock Otterhounds

Of all the many thousands of hunting pictures I have taken, I think that this is probably the most timeless of all. It could have been taken at almost any time during the Culmstock's long history (except that there weren't any cameras around at its formation in 1790): the dress, the hounds, the cottage covered in creeper and roses, even the 'old-fashioned' expressions on the faces of the hunt servants, give little clue as to the date. In fact it was taken in June 1973 at the kennels at Reaphay near Taunton before a joint day with the Eastern Counties Otterhounds, who had travelled down to Somerset from their kennels at Maldon in Essex. Master and huntsman of the Culmstock since 1957, Mr Norman Bartlett looks very little different today and he guided his Eastern-Counties' counterpart Mr Stafford Babbage (who has since moved to the West Country) along the river throughout what became a rather damp day's sport. However, I have also had several splendid outings with the Culmstock on its west of England rivers when the sun shone and the water was warm. The hunt staff, resplendent in red coats and waistcoats, topped by French grey bowler hats, leading enormous crowds of keen followers through some of England's most beautiful countryside, whilst hounds drew for an otter. Then, when they found, their cry was tremendous as they swam the deep pools or when the otter took to dry land. Often hunts went on for more than three hours and even the most timid of followers became excited enough to venture into the river, close to the sharp end of the sport.

Since 1978, hounds have turned to hunting that scourge of the river's wildlife, the mink, and whilst the hunts are much shorter, supporters are just as keen and numerous, as they follow those same French grey bowlers along the rivers just as they have done for the past two hundred years.

*The David Davies hounds, with huntsman David Jones and keen foot-followers Edward and Jackie Harris, marking to ground 1600 feet up in the hills of Montgomeryshire.*

# The David Davies, Montgomeryshire

Still very much a family pack, this hunt was founded in 1905 by David Davies, later Lord Davies, and the present Lord, although he no longer hunts hounds, remains very much 'the boss', and field master on Saturdays. His eldest daughter, Eldrydd, is extremely keen too and helps at the kennels when home from school. She also goes like a bomb across country, not only out hunting, but also at horse trials in the summer. David Davies stallion hounds are used throughout Wales and one very active bitch called Velvet has gone to the Isle of Wight to start a most successful outcross in a very different type of country.

For years I had read with interest reports on this, 'the premier Welsh pack', but it was not until November 1973 that I made my debut in their marvellous mountainous country in Montgomeryshire, mid-Wales. This was for a mounted day in their flatter vale country close to the river Severn, at Oakley Park. In the very next season I went to Llandinam for a foot day in the rugged and steep hills behind the kennels, with the joint master and huntsman Lord Davies carrying the horn. The weather was appalling yet hounds ran remarkably well and gave us the slip as we couldn't hear even their spine-chilling cry for the gale! After many miles of foot-slogging, when I was guided by Clem and Bryn Richards, two of the keenest supporters, we found hounds marking on a bleak and rocky hillside, at a place which has since became known as 'Jim Meads' earth'.

Little did I realise that ten years later I would move to Wales and the David Davies would become 'my pack'. And what a marvellous place it is to live. Hounds are hunted three days a week on foot, whilst Saturdays give the mounted brigade their chance to follow huntsman David Jones (known locally as 'Dai the hunt') who, with his wife Sue, has run the Llandinam kennels since 1973, providing open house for all comers.

*Huntsman Dennis Boyles with the Devon and Somerset stag-hounds on Exmoor, above War-ren Farm.*

*Hounds in full cry across open moorland.*

# The Devon and Somerset Staghounds

This picture was taken on an unscheduled visit in August 1988. Having been to the Honiton hound show on the Thursday, I decided to stay on for another day and cover the Exmoor's first morning cub-hunting. All went well: hounds moved off at 6.30 a.m. and soon there were several pictures in the bag as hounds began to run at top speed. Suddenly low cloud descended in typical Exmoor fashion, reducing visibility to a few damp yards. Although only a couple of miles from my car, on ground I was familiar with, it took some finding. Undaunted, still feeling full of running and knowing that the Devon and Somerset staghounds were also having their first meet of the autumn season on lower ground, I headed for Warren Gate. Luckily the fog soon cleared and the three joint-masters, Maurice and Diana Scott and Phillip Hawkins, gave the order to move off. Quickly, long-serving huntsman Dennis Boyles had the tufters in action and for the next hour or so I ran across those beautiful moors, being in the right place often enough to enjoy some great views of ten red deer running together. Finally the 'right' stag was separated from his friends and the main pack sent for. Once they were laid on, their cry echoed vibrantly across the heather and combes and after one circle back to Warren Farm they were away and over the horizon! I walked slowly back to the meet, for once at leisure to savour the sights, sounds and smells of Exmoor, before beginning the long drive home.

*Waterford.*

*Examples of ditches and the
problems which they can cause!*

*Westmeath.*

# *Ditches*

I've seen really hard-riding thrusters, who think nothing of jumping big hedges or timber, go quite pale on being confronted by an unnacustomed yawning chasm of a ditch. Add a few feet of water and it becomes even more terrifying to the rider and horse who haven't seen many ditches out hunting. Yet there are places where these provide the majority of jumping and hedges – if there are any – are viewed with suspicion! East Anglia is famous for its ditches: the Berkeley has its rhines whilst in the Holderness and East Middleton I've seen people tackle ditches which look more like an arm of the sea! On my first visit to the Meath hunt, to the north west of Dublin, I was absolutely amazed at the size and depth of some of the machine-excavated ditches. Sure enough, one or two horses found their way into the bottom of these during the hunt and a well-known Brigadier finished with a broken leg. In the past, locals had quite a lucrative time, rescuing horses and riders from such fearsome obstacles for a cash fee – the thought of staying trapped all day usually made the tip quite a generous one! Sadly, the other great danger is to the horse rather than the rider, for I've seen on several occasions a horse not quite clear the spread of the ditch and finish with a broken back as its hind legs hit below the lip – each time the rider was thrown clear. In my selection of pictures of ditches shown here and overleaf, none of the horses or riders was hurt although I got very wet helping the one out of the wet ditch in the Blackmore and Sparkford Vale's country in Dorset, and top flat race jockey George Duffield found that hunting with the West Norfolk was much more dangerous than riding at Newmarket!

37

*Co Louth.*

*West Norfolk.*

*Lincolnshire.*

38

*Co Limerick.*

*Blackmore and Sparkford Vale.*

*Co Tipperary.*

39

*Riders making their way through a field of golden rod and Michaelmas daisies, during a day's hunting in Ontario.*

*Major Charles Kindersley MFH, who has been master since 1949.*

## The Eglinton and Caledon, Ontario, Canada

**H**ave any of you ever seen hounds draw a dazzling field of michaelmas daises and golden rod? Not only draw it, but find a brace of foxes therein and gallop away through it behind the field master? Well I have, and it happened during a day with Canada's Eglinton and Caledon Hunt, formed in 1930. Amazingly, and despite clouds of pollen flying in all directions, these hounds, bred by senior joint-master Major Charles Kindersley from the best Beaufort, Heythrop and Portman blood, were able to hunt, although not hard enough to seriously test their quarry. (Major Kindersley has been a master since 1949 and is reputed to have ordered a new hunting saddle for his eightieth birthday!)

In Canada, because of the severe winters, the hunting season comes in two parts: autumn or fall hunting runs from the heat of August until the big freeze at the end of November, then comes the spring season of April and May. My visit was during the fall of 1980 when the colours of the trees made an unbelievable kaleidoscope of red, brown, gold and yellow, but the ground was bone dry and hard except in a few wild swampy areas alongside a creek. One hazard which we don't encounter in the British Isles is the groundhog, whose overgrown burrows cause many unpleasant falls for horse and riders. There were also thick woodlands to give foxes cover and we found two-and-a-half brace during the day: however, scent was poor although hounds hunted accurately and marked a brace to ground before 'home' was blown at 5 o'clock.

*One of Welsh hunting's great characters, Mr Pyrs Williams MFH, with hounds on Snowdon.*

# The Eryri,
# Wales

Ask any hunting person to name the most rugged hunting country in Britain and the majority would suggest one of the fell packs in Cumbria. I have my doubts and put forward the Eryri as the toughest, including as it does much of the Snowdonia National Park and Snowdon itself, soaring to 3560 feet above sea level. They also hunt in Anglesey but that is on much more level ground and nowhere near as challenging. Formed initially in 1968, as a harrier pack by that great character Pyrs Williams, the Eryri soon turned to chasing the fox at the request of local farmers, most of whom run flocks of sheep in very wild country. Those big, tough and resourceful mountain foxes would soon dent the farmer's profits at lambing time, so hunting is essential to the area's prosperity. Pyrs Williams built kennels at his Nantgwynant farm, where a sheer unclimbable rock face on one side keeps in even the most active Welsh foxhound who are not put off by a six-foot high fence. A lovely, true story is told about Pyrs. A lady, asking how she would recognise him, was told, 'Look for a wiry man with a face like a Welsh Fox. She soon found him!

In 1983 Richard Williams was appointed to hunt hounds for his grandfather, four years later he became a joint master and has proved to be a real chip off the old block, to the great delight of Pyrs (who sadly died in 1988). Happily, the pack which he founded is in excellent hands and carries on the family tradition of which he was so proud.

*Captain Ronnie Wallace MFH amidst typical Exmoor scenery.*

# The Exmoor, Devon

A long with hundreds of thousands of other people, I love Exmoor. In the winter it is often more than inhospitable, with its bitter winds, sudden fogs, rain or snow, yet in the autumn and spring when the sun is shining and the air is clear, it's heaven. The patchwork of cultivated fields, the heather-clad moorland, the deep, mysterious combes, the rivers, the huge skies and soaring buzzards colour a landscape of unforgettable beauty and grandeur. When I began my career in 1950 one of the first 'long way away' hunts I travelled to was the Exmoor. In those days the amazing Lt Col Guy Jackson was master – and I mean amazing, because he rode across the moor with the best of them despite having lost both legs during the war. His huntsman was Victor Martin, a real character who knew the country like the back of his hand, whilst the whipper-in carried a terrier in a satchel on his back, as four-wheel drive vehicles were still few and far between. In 1956 Jack Hosegood left the nearby Minehead Harriers to become a joint master, taking over the horn in 1964 when Victor retired and hunting hounds with distinction for thirteen seasons. In 1969 the hunt celebrated the centenary of its foundation by Nicholas Snow, who called it originally 'The Stars of the West'.

1977 witnessed a big change at the Exmoor: after an epic twenty-five years mastership of the Heythrop, Captain Ronnie Wallace moved west and became their joint master and huntsman. Soon, from being just a 'little farmer's pack', it became *the* fashionable place to go hunting as the season on the moors extends from early August until May. The breeding of the hounds developed enormously and soon many championships were being won and Exmoor stallions began to be used all over the world. Today, visitors flock to Exmoor, not only to enjoy the countryside but to watch a great pack of hounds being handled by that phenomenon of twentieth-century foxhunting, Captain Ronnie Wallace.

*This and next pages: A sample of the obstacles which are jumped out hunt and some results.*

Top: *Heythrop.*
Left: *Mr Michael Dempsey MFH – East Galway.*
Above: *Meynell.*

# Fences and Falls

M any people simply hunt for the ride rather than for the pleasure of watching hounds at work. For them the interest comes in negotiating whatever obstacle appears in front of them, and many count the fences they jump during a day and judge its success accordingly. One of the excitements of the chase in Great Britain is that the followers are never quite sure what is round the next corner or on the other side of the field. Certain hunts and the country they cover are recognisable by their obstacles. For example, the Galway Blazers and the High Peak Harriers are noted for their stone walls which, surrounding small grass enclosures, can present themselves at the rate of one a minute. In contrast, the shires of High Leicestershire are mostly timber or thorn hedges, but with plenty of ditches to catch out the unwary. Then again, packs which hunt in East Anglia, and the Meath, near to Dublin, are proper 'ditch' countries, whilst the Berkeley have their 'rhines'. In the far west of England, on the other hand, where such hunts as the Four Burrow and those of Cornwall operate, banks predominate – as they do in many places in Ireland such as Waterford, Kilkenny and Wexford, whilst the Limerick country has both banks and walls. Nowadays many obstacles are topped by wire, which makes life more hazardous but of course there are always people who will fly these freely, as they would iron railings, five-barred gates and cattle troughs. They remind us that we hunt for fun, so enjoy yourselves, but occasionally look before you leap, for it is not unheard of to jump out of a field, onto a road and land on a car!

Here is my selection of the successful and the less successful.

*A broken leg in Virginia USA (The Warrenton) gets immediate attention.*

*Vale of Aylesbury.*

*Mrs Janet Spratt – Berkeley.*

*Mr Robin Cursham – Blackmore and Sparkford Vale.*

*Mr Billy McKeever MFH – Co Louth.*

*Mr Bobby Barry – Co Tipperary.*

*Emily Preston – Bicester.*

*Mrs Rosemary Samworth MFH – Cottesmore.*

1 *Mr Brod Munro-Wilson – Quorn.*    2 *Mrs Charlotte Rodrigues – Quorn.*
3 *Mrs Jane Hankey – Cheshire Forest.*    4 *Mr Dick Brake – Taunton Vale.*
5 *Lady Wills – Heythrop.*    6 *Mr David Meynell MFH – Meynell.*
7 *Godfrey Berry – Romney Marsh.*    8 *Mr Duncan Douglas – Cheshire Forest.*

9 *South Notts.*    10 *Captain Tom Morgan MFH – West Waterford.*    11 *Portman.*
12 *Mr David Naylor-Leyland – Quorn.*    13 *Llangibby.*
14 *The Hon Mallowry Spens – East Kent.*

The Fernie's long-serving
huntsman Bruce Durno leading
hounds to draw Shangton Holt
covert.

Joint master Mr Alan Hinch on
his sweating horse during a good
hunt.

# The Fernie,
# Leicestershire

The coverts Gumley, Walton, Shangton Holt, the Laughton Hills and Jane Ball all hold precious memories for me of splendid sport with the Fernie hounds, a pack first formed in 1853. However, my all-time favourite in their country is John Ball from where, on almost every occasion, one of the resident foxes goes away in the right direction, thus giving the mounted field a great ride across the old turf and thorn hedges of the Saddington Vale. Thanks to the Cowen family, particularly Joe Cowen who has been joint master since 1972, this marvellous area of hunting country has been retained as permanent grazing land and not turned over to corn, with consequent loss of wildlife. My earliest visit came in 1950 when Walter Gupwell had just taken over the huntsman's post, and sharing the mastership were the Colonels Hignett and Lloyd. Then, from the Quorn came the towering figure of Lt Col Tony Murray-Smith, who hunted hounds with Bruce Durno in charge of the kennels at Great Bowden. Since 1965, Bruce has carried the horn, hunting his colourful pack of hounds with great zest, and he is fortunate to have a settled mastership for Alan Hinch and Rod Millington joined Joe Cowen in 1983. Another notable figure who did so much to keep the Fernie at the top of the league was Dick Watson who was honorary secretary from 1941 to 1989. When he retired, two people took over his job!

On the day that I took this picture, in January 1983, the meet was at Shangton where the weather was still, grey and bitterly cold. An enormous field decided it was a day not to be missed, and they were right. As always, Shangton Holt held, and the first fox was hunted westwards towards Carlton Curlieu, turning north to Illston on the Hill. Another hunt went past Ashland towards Billesdon, then eastwards across the main road to Skeffington Vale and to Rolleston. In fact hounds flew all day until dusk, to the delight of the riders which included Fife Symington from the Green Spring Valley Hunt in Maryland, U.S.A.

# The Field Master

Occasionally, during a day's hunting, when things have not gone quite right for the riders, one hears a comment such as 'That idiotic field master got us left at the covert side and we missed the best hunt of the day!' Sadly, few people give praise to this much–maligned person on the other days when things have gone perfectly. It is a desperately difficult post to fill, needing as it does someone who is brave enough to give the field a lead, knows the country like the back of their hand, avoids unnecessary damage yet at the same time gives the mounted field an entertaining ride. He – or she – spends much time on non-hunting days visiting the area to be ridden over and checking with farmers regarding any new hazard or fresh place from which the mounted field should be kept away. Over the years I have watched and photographed many of these field masters, including some brilliant ones such as Col Jack Lowther of the Pytchley, Maj Dermot Daly of the Heythrop and Dorian Williams of the Whaddon Chase. In more recent times, I've admired people such as Jim Bealby of the Quorn – pictured here – Joss Hanbury of the Cottesmore, Robert Henson and John Blakeway of the Belvoir – Ernie Fenwick of the Zetland, Wendy Evans at the Worcestershire and Richard Sumner at the Heythrop, all of whom give their large fields of thrusters a great ride, yet keep them out of trouble.

Top: *Quorn field master Mr Jim Bealby MFH leading the way near Muxlow Hill.*
Centre left: *Mr Richard Sumner MFH of the Heythrop.*
Centre right: *Miss Wendy Evans MFH of the Worcestershire.*
Bottom: *Mr Ernie Fenwick of the Zetland.*

*The Fife's joint master and huntsman, Mr John Gilmour, with hounds on their way to draw Dunbog, after the bicentenary meet in 1986.*

*Mr John Gilmour MFH.*

# The Fife,
# Scotland

In 1986 the Fife Hunt celebrated its bicentenary and I was more than delighted to be asked to attend their celebratory dinner at Anstruther where the kilt was much in evidence, as indeed were trophies of the chase. The morning after dawned bright, with a chill wind and a white frost, as joint master John Gilmour and kennel huntsman Ian Scholes brought hounds to a spectacularly beautiful meet at Lindores on the shores of the loch. Leading a large number of mounted and car followers, hounds were taken to draw the vast expanses of marshland at Dunbog. I noted all the signs and decided on which side of the bog to proceed. Hounds soon found and quickly left the covert on the 'wrong' side and raced up into the hills. Not wishing to waste time by backtracking round the marsh, I ventured across, treading carefully on solid tussocks of grass. All went well until I was within thirty feet of terra firma when the ground gave way under my weight and I sank in black stinking slime up to my waist! Eventually I reached the far side, by which time I was frozen, so I made better than usual speed to catch the hounds, although I was afraid that they might hunt *me*, steaming and smelly as I was from my exertions! A busy day ensued, on a poor scent, amidst wonderful Scottish scenery with the field having lots of jumping and galloping on grassy hills. Just for once I was delighted when 'home' was blown; even so it was 6 o'clock before I was able to sink into a much-needed hot bath to remove the caked-on mud.

Top left: *A brace of foxes at play in a garden in the Cottesmore country.*
Top right: *A Tynedale fox.*
Centre left: *A fox being hunted by the Mid-Devon about to go to ground.*
Centre right: *An Atherstone fox leaving covert in a hurry.*
Left: *A Cottesmore fox going away.*
Above: *A Duhallow fox crossing a ditch.*

# *Foxes*

Foxes really are the most amazing animals and stories of their cunning are told worldwide. I've seen a fox leave a covert, in which hounds are speaking, lazily trot half way across a field and stop to relieve himself, before moving on in front of the pack: he knew that it was a bad scenting day better than we did. On another day, hounds had checked by a small clump of trees and were at a complete loss; suddenly, the fox jumped out of a thick lime tree amongst the pack who were so astonished that he made good his escape, much to the chagrin of their huntsman.

The two largest pictures which I use opposite could not have been taken in more different circumstances: the top one was shot on an exposed rocky outcrop in the middle of Dartmoor, whilst I took the second one sitting up in bed on a Sunday morning. In the first the Mid-Devon had met at South Zeal and drew on to the moor, hunting round places like Belstone Tor. Then hounds picked up a drag and were away, leaving me toiling up the steep hills and through the heather in their wake. Intuition told me where to go and as I stopped on a rocky knoll to survey the scene I spotted the fox coming towards me. As I was squatting down and perfectly still, he didn't see me and, unbelievably, went to ground under the rocks on which I was standing. The bedroom shot was taken in Cottesmore country at the lovely home of that great hunting lady Betty Cross, with whom I was staying for Burghley horse trials. Looking out of the window at 8 a.m. I couldn't believe my eyes when I saw two foxes on the lawn. Rapidly fitting the telephoto lens to my camera, and finding that there was just enough light, I took three pictures through the window before they ran off and I returned to bed.

*Plenty of action from horses and hounds during a day's hunting in Dorset with the Blackmore and Sparkford Vale. Trevor Winslade in the lead.*

## Full Cry! The Blackmore and Sparkford Vale, Dorset

Intuition, sixth sense, luck – call it what you will, it certainly worked for me with a vengeance during a Foxford visit to the Blackmore and Sparkford Vale in Dorset. The meet was held, on a damp February morning in 1980, at Stalbridge Park, home of the hunt chairman Mr Richard de Pelet whose father, Count Guy de Pelet, was joint master of the Blackmore Vale from 1959 until 1974 following their amalgamation with the Sparkford Vale Harriers in 1971. Interestingly, in those days there were three joint masters who all wore different-coloured coats: Count Guy de Pelet wore red, Lt. Commander Sudlow continued with the green of the harriers, whilst Miss Bridget Holmes A' Court hunted in a smart blue coat with shiny buttons. On this particular day the joint master, Mr Tony Austin, was carrying the horn with his kennel huntsman Tony Herring and the irrepressible Dawn Pinney whipping-in. Hounds found close to the meet and hunted locally before their fox left the park and crossed the main A30 road into Broadsoles covert. A good cast had them running into Martin's Copse and Fuzzy Bushes where they fresh found and raced away over the grand old turf to the Templecombe road where hounds split. Most went in a circle back to Martin's Copse and then on the West Wood; crossing the railway, they hunted the line out to Stowell Spinney from where the hounds twisted and turned with their fox which was marked to ground in the Everlands coverts. It was during this fine hunt, which included a four-mile point, that my intuition had to work overtime, hounds had left me behind and the horses had disappeared, yet an inner voice insisted, 'Keep on running but bear more to the right.' After twenty minutes I was beginning to have my doubts when I heard that magic sound of hounds in fully cry. Soon they were in view and I took one of my favourite pictures of hounds running and, as a fantastic bonus, I also captured the front rank led by joint master Mr Trevor Winslade jumping a huge hedge and ditch with great aplomb.

*Mr Anthony Martyn MFH with the Glamorgan pack on the beach at Merthyr-Mawr, at the end of his last day as huntsman.*

# The Glamorgan

'Since I became master in 1961, the Glamorgan's huntable country has shrunk by a third, with motorways and urbanisation taking the biggest toll.' At the end of his last day as huntsmen, 10 March 1986, this is how Mr Anthony Martyn described to me the changes which had taken place in their smallish country to the west of Cardiff during the hunt's 113-year history. However, there are still areas which are wild, isolated and unspoiled, where hounds can hunt their fox without hindrance. Although this is a Welsh pack, hounds are bred very much on 'establishment' lines, through the Heythrop, Duke of Beaufort's and Berkeley, whilst an outcross back to old English blood has taken place, using the Limerick hound Seaman '76.

The meet, on this end-of-season day, was at Tythegston where Mr Martyn and his wife Fiona, a joint master since 1980, were soon engulfed in a throng of well-wishers, before the order was given to move off. A fox was found in a gorse-covered valley and hunted on a twisty line almost to Porthcawl, with the field jumping wire on the way, before returning to the higher ground where the pack was stopped in dense hill fog. The last hunt of the day began in an amazing area of sand dunes at Merthyrmawr from which the fox did not venture too far and the season ended with hounds checking on the beach, always a spectacular sight, with the field wishing their huntsman 'good night'.

*Mr Johnnie Andrews MH up with his pack, as they find a strong hare, high in the hills of mid-Wales.*

# The Glyn Celyn Beagles, Wales

In 1956 Mr C N de Courcy-Parry, better known as that tremendous hunting character 'Dalesman', brought his pack of hard-hunting beagles back into Wales and reformed the Glyn Celyn, which had been in abeyance since the war. 'Dalesman's beagles' were originally the Clun Forest and showed great sport in the same country as the Montgomery Harriers, of which he was also a master. Later he took them to Cumberland and named them the Caldbeck Fell Beagles. (Rumour has it that he chose this name, with the same initials as the previous pack, so that he could use his original hunt buttons, thus saving money!) In 1958 he was joined in the mastership by Lt Col Tony Jervis for one season before he retired. Mrs Jervis then became a joint master with her husband (one of the last of that dying breed of beaglers who wear shorts) until 1971 when Mr Johnnie Andrews was appointed huntsman, and then a joint master, this partnership continuing into the 1990s. Carrying on the family pack tradition, Johnnie's wife Sarah, whom I first met when she was a whipper-in to the Northern Counties Otterhounds with her great friend June Paisley, has been honorary secretary for the past eleven seasons.

The Glyn Celyn have a marvellous country in Brecon and Radnorshire – mostly grass, with numerous sheep farms, and some really magnificent mountain moorland country where hounds cover a tremendous distance on unspoiled and good scenting ground. This picture was taken on a bright, breezy and chilly day in February 1987, after a well-attended invitation meet at Tyn-y-Cwm. In this picture hounds have just put up a hare in the heather and rushes close to the lakes at Bwlch-y-Garreg and they were soon into their stride. With a great cry they hunted up and down and round, until they caught their hare, to set a new record tally for the pack.

*Leading hounds from the 150th opening meet is whipper-in Matthew Puffer. Behind him rides joint master and huntsman Mr Stephen Lambert.*

*A nasty fall with the Heythrop.*

# *The Heythrop, Oxfordshire*

For decades the Dukes of Beaufort hunted an enormous country extending from Bristol to Oxford. However, in 1835 the eastern part became a separate hunt called the Heythrop, named after the village where the hounds used to be kennelled when they were away from Badminton. A strong link was maintained and the Duke of Beaufort's green livery is still worn by the masters and hunt staff. Therefore it gave me great pleasure and a real sense of occasion to be present at the 150th opening meet, held on November 6th 1985 in the picturesque Cotswold village of Oddington. A large crowd had gathered to see hounds and to listen to several speeches, before joint master and huntsman Mr Stephen Lambert gave the order to move off for a busy day's sport – although scenting conditions were poor. Amongst the speakers was Captain Ronnie Wallace whose brilliant twenty-five years at the helm of the Heythrop from 1952–77 dominates the hunt's history in the second part of the twentieth century. His breeding policy began when he used Portman stallion hounds, such as Playfair and Wizard, on long established Heythrop female lines. This produced many influential foxhounds such as Harper '53; Brigand '54; Choirboy '56; and Craftsman '62 whose names appear in many distinguished pedigrees to this day. In 1988 Stephen Lambert and Tony Collins, who had been in charge of the Chipping Norton kennels since 1970, both retired and Anthony Adams returned to the Heythrop as huntsman. A quartet of masters share control, the longest serving being an amazing lady, Mrs Valerie Willes, now in her 15th season and going as well as ever, despite a bone breaking fall in February 1991. Her joint masters are Mr Richard Sumner, a top-class field master; Mr Peter Stoddart who was a joint master of the Whaddon Chase 1969–83 and Mrs Bunny Scaramanga.

*Amateur huntsman Mr Martin
Brocklehurst jumping a typical
Derbyshire wall.*

# The High Peak Harriers, Derbyshire

Even though I have spent many happy, but hard, days with the High Peak Harriers, formed in 1848, I can remember my first ever visit as though it were yesterday. It was in 1953, during the mastership of those incredible, identical, side-saddle-riding twins, the Misses May and Violet Wilson, with George Steele carrying the horn and Bryan Pheasey (later to achieve fame at the Bicester) as whipper-in. The meet was at The Bull i' the Thorn, a desolate place some 1000 feet above sea level and the rain was cold and torrential from beginning to end. However, it doesn't always rain in the Peak District and when the skies are clear this is one of the most spectacular hunting countries in England. It is nearly all grass, with small fields enclosed by white limestone walls, usually without gates; the hills are steep in places, so one need a fit horse with knee pads, as the whole day is spent jumping, even when hounds are drawing. Hares are strong and plentiful so a busy day is almost guaranteed and over the years I have seen several foxes also found and hunted, even though there is not very much holding cover.

From 1985 to 1989 John Brocklehurst was master with his son Martin carrying the horn most successfully, until pressure of business caused them both to retire, temporarily one hopes. It was during this spell of family control that this picture was taken, in February 1989, following a lawn meet at Middleton Hall, a few miles south of Bakewell. A strong south-westerly wind made conditions difficult and it hardly got light enough to take pictures, yet those stud book harriers and their huntsman gave the large, well-mounted field a splendid day. I managed to be in the right place on a fair number of occasions and was delighted with the results. However, there was a sting in the tail as I finished up soaked to the skin, just as I had on my first visit all those years before.

## HRH The Prince of Wales

I enjoy every day I go hunting, but some I enjoy more than others. Then there are the 'special' ones, such as when I arrive at the meet and the senior master, almost secretively, walks up to me and says, 'You've certainly picked the right day to hunt with us as the Prince of Wales is joining us at the first covert.' This is guaranteed to make the adrenalin flow and the legs to run just a little faster. Since I first met the Prince in 1977 with the Cottesmore, our paths have crossed on numerous occasions and I've been fortunate to photograph him jumping all sorts of fences, a selection of which I reproduce here. In those early days he had his share of falls by being too brave for his lack of hunting experience. I well remember one real 'purler' when the Prince was brought down by wire on the landing side of a big thorn hedge in Cheshire. The remainder of the field, being unsighted, continued to jump the fence, fortunately without landing on His Royal Highness's breathless body. Quickly he learnt to adapt his style to the hunting field, and to slip his reins at the many drop fences encountered in the Quorn and Belvoir countries. Now the Prince is as good as anyone, and better than most across country, and rides upsides top professional huntsmen like Michael Farrin, Robin Jackson, Johnnie O'Shea and David Barker, seldom muddying his coat. It is obvious that His Royal Highness enjoys not only the challenge of hunting, but also the opportunity it gives him to meet farmers and other grass-roots country folk in their own environment. Equally clearly, his presence in the hunting field gives a great many people a tremendous amount of pleasure. Long may your hunting career continue, Sir.

Top: *HRH The Prince of Wales in action with the Quorn.*
Centre left: *Meynell.*   Centre right: *Cheshire.*   Bottom left: *Belvoir.*

*Eglinton huntsman Guy
Sanderson lands a 3lb trout on
Rutland Water, watched by
George Adams from the
Fitzwilliam.*

*A hunt staff cricket team.*

# *Huntsman's Summer*

One of the questions most often asked of a huntsman is 'What on earth do you find to do all summer when there isn't any hunting?' People who hunt all winter tend to forget that the hounds and horses, who have largely been responsible for their enjoyment, still need looking after and their batteries recharged for the forthcoming season. Work in kennels is literally never finished. Apart from the day-to-day chores of flesh collection, skinning and feeding, summer is also the time to refurbish buildings. Neither can the future of the pack be neglected; life becomes especially hectic in the days leading up to the puppy show for the young entry has to be given showing practice, prepared and all their names learned. Throughout the summer, hounds are exercised by the hunt staff on foot, on bicycles of uncertain ancestry, or later on horses so that they are fit to run on the first day of autumn hunting.

'Yes, but what do you do for *fun*?' is another good question. One answer is that many hunt staff enjoy fishing as a total change from the hustle and bustle of hunting. Indeed, a hunt staff fishing match takes place each year on the wide expanses of Rutland Water, where this picture was taken, and splendid trophies are at stake. The other very popular summer sport is cricket, and many hunts run their own teams with home and away fixtures. For years I had my own cricket team which played matches against representative hunt staff teams and, for the record, the very last wicket of the hundreds I took during my long career was that of the Heythrop huntsman Anthony Adams, caught by Captain Brian Fanshawe of the Cottesmore.

*The Isle of Wight hounds puzzling out the line, helped by Mr Michael Poland MFH.*

*Viewing the fox away, as the first two hounds hit off the line.*

## The Isle of Wight

I always enjoy going overseas for a hunting visit, even on the short trip to the Isle of Wight (although I must admit that the ferry crossing is more pleasurable in June en route to the puppy show, than in the depths of winter). The first foxes were imported into the Isle of Wight in the 1820s and the hunt was formed in 1845, replacing the Crockford Harriers which had flourished until then. Their present kennels, built in 1927 at Gatcombe, are almost in the centre of the country. Over the years, locals and 'Oveners' (visitors from the mainland) have enjoyed their sport on the island. Although towns and roads are beginning to encroach on the unspoilt rural areas, hunting folk will still find a great variety of country, including grass, arable, downland, woods and hidden gorse-clad valleys away from the holiday resorts.

Since the war there have been some noted hound men in charge of the Isle of Wight, including Arthur Dalgety, John Dix and John Kingswell (1962–83), since when Michael Poland has been master, and his hounds have won first prizes at Peterborough and other major hound shows. This good-looking pack also hunt well, as I saw on my visit in 1985 when the meet was at The Hare and Hounds, Downend. The master was carrying the horn and the first fox was hunted perseveringly almost to Newport and marked to ground. A second was short-running but the third was a much more ambitious quarry, giving a very fast run. Finding in Combley Hanging, I saw them away on his brush, through Chilling Wood and Pondcast and onto open farmland towards Ryde Airport. He crossed the road by the Ponda Rosa and the terrier man and I just managed to stop hounds as they approached the electric railway with only kennel huntsman Nigel Cox anywhere near, after a racing forty minutes and a four-mile point.

*The end of a brilliant fourteen-mile hunt. With the Jed Forest pack are the master Mr Walter Jeffrey and huntsman Derek Cheetham.*

# The Jed Forest,
# Scotland

ounded in 1884, the Jed Forest Hunt's country is in Scotland around Hawick
and Jedburgh, where there are rocky hills, heather-covered moors and, on
the lower ground, grazing meadows and some arable. I remember having an
excellent day in 1971 from Oxnam with one of the Jed Forest's greatest masters,
the much-loved Roly Harker, who showed great sport and introduced an element
of fell blood into the pack between 1949 and 1978.

To celebrate the Jed Forest's first hundred years Foxford and I were invited to
their centenary festivities at Kelso. The next morning, when many heads were still
thumping following the most successful dinner and dance, huntsman Derek
Cheetham and the master, Walter Jeffrey of the wonderful 'side burns', brought
hounds to the meet at Cavers. A large field enjoyed the crisp winter sunshine which
lit the surrounding hills with a kaleidoscope of late-autumn colour. Hounds soon
found in Kirkton Moss and raced away uphill to Earlside. Horses were struggling
against the gradient to keep in touch and then had trouble galloping down again
although it was all on old turf. Finally, after a brilliant hunt of just under two hours
covering fourteen miles, much of it over wild moorland border country, the fox was
marked to ground at Whitriggs, watched by the few followers still in the chase.

*Jersey's Trinity Manor makes a splendid background for Major John Riley and his West-country harriers.*

*Joint master Mr Stephen Arthur jumping a wall built during the German occupation.*

# *The Jersey Island Draghunt*

Having played cricket on the holiday island of Jersey, for David Nicholson's national hunt team, I found it difficult to visualise the countryside with its teeming crowds of tourists as suitable hunting terrain. Yet, there I was flying in to Jersey's airport in late November 1982 to find the island almost empty and the wintry landscape looking vastly different. Surprisingly, there are no foxes, despite the long-term involvement with the British Army (who, incidentally, introduced the red fox to America) so a drag is substituted. The hunt was formed by officers of the British garrison battalions in the late nineteenth century and, apart from the duration of the two world wars, has continued ever since. Foxhounds, beagles and harriers were all tried, but the latter proved most suitable and kennel huntsman William Headdon's pack has many West-Country harriers, bred by his father George at the North Norfolk. Hounds are kennelled at the beautiful, chateau-like Trinity Manor, home of Major John Riley – joint master and huntsman who has shared control with Stephen Arthur since 1962 – and hunt two days a week.

There is tremendous support for this island pack so numbers of riders have to be limited and a strong field master is a necessity, otherwise damage would soon be done to the large areas of market garden and flower-growing fields. A day's hunting will cover about nine miles over a varied terrain, with small hedges, banks and timber, although on the day I was out some members jumped obstacles left over from the German occupation in the 1940s which remain as museum pieces to that unhappy part of Jersey's history.

*Major Victor McCalmont, the Kilkenny's master since 1949, on one of his last days hunting hounds.*

*Sir William Blunden in action.*

## The Kilkenny,
## Ireland

In 1921 the famous American foxhunter and hound breeder *extraordinaire* Mr Ikey Bell retired after a thirteen-year mastership of the Kilkenny hunt, formed in 1797. Control was taken over by Major Dermot McCalmont who built new kennels on his marvellous estate at Mount Juliet near Thomastown, on the banks of a noted salmon river, the Nore. In 1949 he was joined in the mastership by his son, Major Victor McCalmont, who remains as senior master into the 1990s. They have bred a notable pack of hounds which not only hunt well but are good-looking too – indeed, one of the loudest cheers I have ever heard at the Peterborough Royal Foxhound Show came in 1978 when Kilkenny Famous '77 won the bitch championship. Their country is beautiful, wild and undulating with plenty of grass. Yet it is a great challenge to cross when hounds run for the obstacles, which include stone walls, banks, ditches and fly fences. You need a clever horse as in places rocks abound (particularly in an area ominously named Murder Mile!). Everybody who hunts has to go well and jump – there can be no creeping about on roads – so horses and riders which have followed the Kilkenny are sure to be able to hunt anywhere successfully. This picture, taken in December '83, has a touch of sadness about it for, because of illness, it was almost the last time that Major Victor McCalmont was able to carry the horn. That evening we had a marvellous dinner party at Mount Juliet presided over by the fun-loving Mrs Bunny McCalmont, who was so tragically killed out hunting a couple of years later.

*With the Eildon Hills in the background, the Lauderdale's kennel huntsman, Michael King, collects his pack at the end of a long day.*

*Mr Chris Spalding MFH about to fall into a ditch on the landing side of this big wall.*

## *The Lauderdale,*
## *Scotland*

Hunting the fox in those wild countries of the Scottish borders has an atmosphere all of its own. The Lauderdale's terrain is hilly but with lots of old turf, including huge areas of 'white' grass, well-fenced or walled and far fewer people hunting than would be the case if this landscape was further south. The master and huntsman, Mr Chris Spalding, commutes on hunting days from North Yorkshire where he farms whilst an old friend of mine from his Fernie days, Michael King is in charge at the kennels close to Lauder. Often the weather can be harsh in the extreme and many days are lost to frost or snow, but the welcome given to visitors is as warm as you'll find anywhere. However, we were to be lucky on our visit in November 1979 for the sun shone on the gathering of hounds and riders at Threepwood. Despite the sun, there was a holding scent and a big fox was soon away across those big fields from Cushie Wood. The pack was hot on his brush as he crossed Laings Bog to Upper Blainslie and to Jeniefield Farm and Langshaw where they checked. A good cast soon had hounds back on the line to Moss House Farm and Chatto Crags. It was during this part of the hunt, whilst I was running close to the master, that he jumped a huge wall in fine style, only to take a sickening fall into a unsuspected ditch on the landing side. Unhurt and quickly back into the saddle, Mr Spalding was in touch to help his hounds over the only ploughed field they met, until, after a twelve-mile run in eighty minutes with a four-mile point, hounds were stopped because of shooting arrangements. A couple of short hunts concluded the day with 'home' being blown and the pack collected on a steep grassy hillside overlooking a deep valley, with the impressive Eildon Hills silhouetted against the evening sky.

*The 'Old English' hounds of the
County Limerick Hunt on their
way to draw a gorse covert.*

## The County Limerick, Ireland

What a wealth of marvellous memories this picture conjures up! Leading the pack of Old English hounds, first formed in 1825, to a fresh draw on a typical 'soft' day in January in the County Limerick's wall country is Paddy Regan, kennel huntsman 1946–71. Next comes one of foxhunting's all-time great characters, Lord Daresbury, master of the Belvoir 1934–47 and then master of the Limerick 1947–80 – where he carried the horn like a professional from 1947 until 1972, when Hugh Robards took over. Completing the trio is second whipper-in Miss Meriel Atkinson, another tremendous character who hunted with Lord Daresbury for fifty years and was brilliant at crossing the country and seeing a fox. The country is really challenging, with banks, ditches and walls in abundance and, with very little plough to slow the pace, riders have to 'kick on or get left'.

I shall never forget my first meeting with Lord Daresbury: it was during the terrible winter of 1962–3 and the setting a smart dinner party at the home of Captain Evan Williams MFH, in Tipperary. We were correctly attired in dinner jackets when the door opened and the noble lord was ushered in, resplendent in a bright red tracksuit! On a later occasion, at the end of a very hard day's hunting with the County Limerick, I told him that I had taken a lovely picture showing his exhausted kennel huntsmen and worn-out horses surrounded by tired hounds. His reply was straight to the point: 'Young man, my hounds *never* get tired!'

*Two foxes which lived dangerously – one did and one didn't!*

## *Living Dangerously*

This is a tale of two foxes, one of which has a happy ending whilst the other does not, depending on where your sympathies lie.

The top picture was taken during a day with the Burton Hunt following their opening meet at Torksey. Formed in 1672, since the last war the Burton have become very much a family pack: from 1949 Mr William Lockwood was a joint master; in 1959 his son Arthur took office, in 1981 his grandson John joined his father in the mastership and under their guidance the hunt has gone from strength to strength. Jim Lang has carried the horn since 1967, and he had put hounds in to draw a covert when I took this all-action shot. I was standing on a central ride when a fox appeared from my left and hounds from the right. Quickly into top gear, Charlie pulled away from his pursuers, leaving the wood and crossing arable fields into a rough area where, despite many twists and turns, those sharp hounds added him to their tally.

The lower picture was taken during a day with my home pack, the David Davies, from a midweek foot meet at The Glyn. A mixed pack of Welsh and Fell hounds had marked a fox to ground high in the hills around the 1600-foot contour, with just the huntsman David Jones and myself in attendance. A few more puffing and sweating followers arrived then, whilst we waited for the terriers, the fox bolted. With the pack on his brush, this strong fox raced downhill through the bracken, reaching the first sheep netting in front of the flying hounds, who were in splendid voice. Gaining a few yards at this fence and the next two, Charlie reached the wooded gullies below and, using all his guile, extended his lead. After a super-fast fifty-minute hunt, the pack lost him: The huntsman was not pleased, but I gave a little cheer and wished that brave fox *bon voyage*.

*Mandy Pritchard, who has carried the Llangeitho's horn since 1987, with hounds on old turf.*

# *The Llangeitho (Mr Dix's),*
# *Wales*

Carrying the horn with a pack of foxhounds has been almost entirely a male prerogative, certainly as a professional. Of course I can recall lady masters such as Mrs Douglas-Pennant (Dartmoor), Mrs Mitchell (Hambledon), The Duchess of Newcastle (Wylye Valley), Lady Waechter (North Ledbury) and Mrs Fagan and Mrs Wallace (South Shropshire) hunting their own hounds. However, until the arrival of Rachel Green at the Monmouthshire Foxhounds, I can't find any other record of a professional female huntsman. Thus it was something of an occasion when I attended the opening meet of the Llangeitho Hunt in November '88 to see Mandy Pritchard begin her second season as a professional huntsman. Riding a thoroughbred point-to-pointer, Passion Play, Mandy looked every inch the part in her red coat and she blows the horn as well as any man. An excellent day's hunting followed in wild, open and hilly country and forestry during which a brace of foxes were caught, to the delight of the very supportive farmers.

The Llangeitho, formed in 1967, is a very much a family pack, run by veteran foxhunter Mr John Dix and his 'two girls', his daughter Julia Hopkins who whips-in and Mandy who carries the horn. With the kennels at home, a few miles from Tregaron in Cardiganshire, all three have to muck in and do the horses and hounds and all the skinning – so it's a hard life, but one which they clearly all love. Mr Dix has kept and hunted hounds all his life – in Ireland, on Dartmoor and the Isle of Wight – and for twenty-five years Mandy has been with him as whipper-in and kennelman and now as huntsman.

The London hunt with hounds on
the shores of Lake Erie.
Left to right *Mrs Elizabeth
Klinger MFH, Derrick Mobey
(huntsman), Dr John
McDonald MFH, and Peter
Andersen (whipper-in).*

*Joint master Mrs Elizabeth
Klinger clearing a typical jump.*

## The London, Ontario, Canada

No, our capital city hasn't gone 'green' and acquired a pack of foxhounds and, despite having the rivers Thames and Medway, and with hunt kennels at Hyde Park, this is London, Ontario. Formed in 1843 by the British army, the pack became civilianised in 1885, since when it has gone from strength to strength. The country seems ideal for hunting, with large woodlands set in rolling farmland and grassy meadows along the river valleys. The whole area has hunt jumps of the post-and-rail or coop varieties, plus a few more natural obstacles. In 1953 Colonel Fuller became master; later he took to carrying the horn, with his daughter Elizabeth as an amateur whipper-in and in 1972 she joined him in office.

At the time of my visit in November 1980, Elizabeth (now Mrs Klinger) and Dr John McDonald, who acts as field master, were in control, with Derrick Mobey as professional huntsman. The meet was by invitation of Colonel John Ker on his Malahide estate, whose house, set on cliffs above the shores of Lake Erie, commands magnificent views over its waters. Staying at the house the night before the meet, we witnessed a storm, with torrential rain and gale force winds which whipped up ten foot waves on the lake. Fortunately, the storm had blown itself out by morning, when hounds gathered on the lawn in front of the house. Thinking that some of them looked familiar, I asked the huntsman about their breeding: 'Oh, they're a draft which Peter Jones sent me from the Pytchley. No wonder! A busy day followed, with one hunt finishing almost in Lake Erie where I took this picture. Back at Malahide after 'home' had been blown and as skeins of greese flew overhead, we were ushered into dinner to the sound of bagpipes, organised by Colonel and Mrs Ker for the pleasure of their guests.

# Lucinda

Horse trials have always been of great interest to me for, although they do not pose quite the same problems for the photographer as a day's hunting, there is always plenty of action! I am not one for sitting on a comfortable chair at a single obstacle all day; for me the challenge is in running round the course, photographing every fence, yet not missing even one 'no-hoper' horse. This I have managed to do in the UK, France, Germany, Switzerland, America and Australia and whilst it was hard work in the often hot weather, it was also a great challenge – and that's what I thrive on.

It was in 1971 at some of the smaller events that I became aware of a most attractive and energetic young lady rider who 'ran' her course walks and plotted her line between fences at the double. The following year I met Lucinda Prior-Palmer officially for the first time, when she won the Midland Bank finals at Cirencester on Be Fair, and have been a great fan of her ever since. Unlike so many other 'stars', Lucinda is just as nice now as she was in 1972, despite her tremendous achievements in horse trials. It has been my privilege and pleasure to have been present at all of her major victories, including her unrivalled six wins at Badminton on different horses, her European championships, her Burghley triumphs and – greatest of all – her World Championship victory at Luhmuhlen on the Australian stock horse Regal Realm. Now she commentates on television and her description of Karen Straker's fall at the Seoul Olympics was brilliant: 'Sit back! *Sit back*! SIT BACK! ------OOOH! SHSSSUGAR!'

*Lucinda Green, on Regal Realm, winning the World Championship in Luhmuhlen, Germany in 1982.*

93

*Joy Slater and Cancottage clear one of the huge fences en route to a unique victory in The Maryland Hunt Cup in 1980.*

Top: *East Essex huntsman John O'Shea taking hounds to draw in their mostly plough country.*

Above: *Mr Edmund Vestey, joint master and huntsman of the Thurlow Hunt, with hounds on stubble during a morning's cub-hunting.*

Above: *Followers of the Cattistock galloping through wet fields at Abbotsbury, whilst swans fly overhead.*

Opposite: *The Duke of Beaufort and his joint master Capt Ian Farquhar with hounds waiting to move off from a meet at Badminton House.*

*Now in his 25th season as huntsman, Stan Luckhurst walking out the West Kent hounds near their kennels at Penshurst.*

Top: *The West Norfolk hounds in a typical East Anglian setting with Ian Higgs, their huntsman for 1981–88.*

Left: *John Nicholson who hunted the Lunesdale from 1963–90 with hounds in rugged Lake District scenery, above the 2,080 foot contour.*

Above: *Veteran huntsman Melvin Poe with the distinctive Orange County Foxhounds in Virginia, USA.*

## The Maryland Hunt Cup, USA

If you haven't been to the Maryland Hunt Cup, America's foremost timber race, then it's time you did. It really is like nothing else in steeplechasing, with horses having to jump twenty-two enormous upright solid wooden fences set in a four-mile course around a pleasant grassy valley north of Baltimore. Small wonder indeed that Jay Trump and Ben Nevis, winners of this tremendously challenging race, have crossed the Atlantic and won the greatest test of all – our Grand National. I have watched the Hunt Cup several times (and seen the local Green Spring Valley Foxhounds on the course) but I shall never forget the first time that I saw those thoroughbred timber-jumpers galloping towards the enormous third fence. 'Surely they'll take a pull,' I said to myself. But no, they just kicked on and sailed over this solid timber fence standing five foot high, a remarkable feat repeated all round the course. Sometimes a horse gets it wrong and falls because those poles don't break – then there are some spectacular photographs!

Amazingly for so prestigous a race, there is a very little in the way of pomp and circumstance: there is a tiny parade ring of chestnut palings, a miniscule canvas changing tent for jockeys, no betting, no bars – so people bring car picnics and their own booze – and no supporting races at all. The day's entertainment lasts for something like nine-and-a-half minutes, yet around 10,000 people attend, come rain or come shine. In 1980 it rained, yet it was a day which went down in the long history of the race for it was won by a lady jockey for the very first time: Jack Griswold, riding in this classic for the twelfth time, tried to make all the running on Beech Prince, but at the last the former Brod Munro-Wilson horse, Cancottage, was urged ahead by Joy Slater for an epic victory.

*The Meynell field galloping uphill during a fast hunt from Okeover Hall.*

*Mr David Pennell MFH 1984–89.*

# *The Meynell,*
# *Derbyshire*

Peter Beckford's advice, 'Take not your hounds out on a very windy day', is one with which I agree, yet on this occasion in January 1984 we were proved wrong. The Meynell, formed in 1816, were meeting at Okeover Hall where Sir Peter Walker-Okeover dispensed much-needed warming hospitality as a bitterly cold gale force wind tore at us continuously and threatened to unseat riders from their horses. Okeover Hall is north of Ashbourne on the edge of the Peak District and close to 1000 feet above sea level, so there was only a limited amount of shelter.

The day began slowly, as all the experts had predicted, with foxes being found in covert but not relishing a run in the open. Then, with a snow squall adding to our discomfort, a good strong fox was found which went away uphill, closely followed by the frozen mounted followers (which is when I took the picture reproduced here). Fly fences and timber soon gave way to stone walls as hounds ran higher, into the wind, on old turf. Marvellous views unfolded on all sides, including the exquisite Dove Valley, as hounds ran brilliantly for over an hour until scent was finally blown away completely.

Taken back to lower ground, we hunted all about Okeover Park and neighbouring coverts until a blizzard at dusk brought to an end this excellent day's hunting in the most appalling conditions where huntsman Graham Roberts and his hounds really earned their keep.

*The hunted fox crossing a ride on a very snowy day with the Middleton.*

*Hounds going home at the end of a snowy day's foot hunting.*

## *The Middleton, Yorkshire*

Throughout my formative years as a hunting photographer, and later, one name was synonymous with the fortunes of the Middleton, that of Lord Irwin (later Lord Halifax) a master from 1946 until 1980. I recall some splendid days when he was hunting hounds, a duty he shared with that most popular of professionals Dennis Sturgeon – in particular one in the hills around Great Givendale which really had me puffing and blowing. The Middleton, formed in 1764, hunts an enormous country; indeed from 1921–53 the Middleton East was run as a separate pack, initially being kennelled at Birdsall, but later with their own establishment at Langtoft, near Driffield.

How well I remember the day in December 1978 when I took this picture – not so much for the hunting but because of the appalling drive to the meet in Yorkshire. There was snow everywhere and a speed limit of 25mph on the M1, yet I made it in time despite much sideways motoring which really set the adrenalin pumping.

David Herring was joint master and huntsman at the time. Conditions were decidedly slippery so the majority of people were on foot, including the hunt staff, which suited me well as I reckoned that I could outrun them! Hounds soon found and began to run on a surprisingly good scent with the fox making his way to a large covert. Anticipating his route, I lay in wait in the snow where I hoped he would cross a well-kept ride. Luck was with me for, a moment or two later, there he was and his picture was in the bag. The figure in the background is that great point-to-point rider Sir Guy Cunard, who also enjoyed his foxhunting.

*A very hot, early-season meet at
Cedar Heights, Georgia, with
Mr Ben Hardaway MFH,
amongst his light-coloured
hounds.*

*Mr Ben Hardaway in action in
Alabama.*

# The Midland, USA

Ask any foxhunting enthusiast about their knowledge of American masters and the vast majority will know, or know about, Ben Hardaway of the Midland, which was formed in 1950 and hunts over the southern states of Georgia and Alabama. He frequently crosses the Atlantic to attend hunting functions or to judge at shows during the summer for he is a most knowledgeable breeder of foxhounds, and this shows with his own pack. Not for Ben the standard American foxhound but a carefully selected cross of the old July hound, fell hounds from the College Valley or West Waterford and a small proportion of Penn-Marydel blood. His pack hunts brilliantly, have marvellous voices and regularly catch foxes, coyotes and bobcats under the guidance of their excitable breeder and huntsman, despite the hot and dry conditions prevalent in the deep south.

Not only is Ben a great hound man but he is also the most entertaining and generous of hosts, and each season he has numerous visitors from the UK to stay and experience hunting with the Midland. In the hottest part of the season, meets are at dawn and shirt sleeves are the order of the day. Once 'home' has been blown, it's time for a super champagne breakfast followed by a lazy afternoon in the swimming pool sipping mint juleeps or gin and tonics. Then, as a special treat, visitors are introduced to 'coon' hunting at night. Trencher-fed coon hounds gather and are loosed off into the darkness with the field hazardously following their cry in pick-up trucks, all wearing fibre-glass leggings as the area abounds with rattlesnakes.

*Mr Derek Jones MH walking hounds back to the meet at the end of an excellent day in the Black Mountains with the Monmouthshire Beagles.*

*A good view helps the beagles on their way.*

## The Monmouthshire Beagles

In 1959 that great hunting character and hound man Derek Jones formed his own pack, the Penhow Mousehounds. Three years later they became the Penhow Beagles and went from strength to strength, with their original name being used as the *nom-de-plume* for the really descriptive and detailed hunt reports which the master penned. At about the same time the adjacent Pandy Beagles were also started, again with tremendous local support, and in 1971 these two packs combined to form the Monmouthshire Beagles. Their large country includes an assortment of grassy vales, big woodlands and many spectacular mountain and moorland areas of the Black Mountains, where the tops are well over 2000 feet and the hares big and strong.

It was with some trepidation that I approached Derek Jones for permission to have a day with his hounds, for the reports told of very long hunts and I was afraid that my legs and lungs would be found wanting! On three occasions I was scheduled to visit a meet at the mountainous village of Craswall, only to be foiled by heavy snow. Eventually, on a fourth date, March 1979, I again set out for Craswall, but a blizzard during the morning thwarted us and hounds had to meet on lower ground near Pandy. However, the scenery, although not as rugged as on the mountains, was pretty. The master was hunting his brilliant pack with Edward and Jackie Harris whipping-in. Despite the snow which lay in many places, a marvellous day's sport followed with hounds in sparkling form and really tremendous voice. Many miles were covered and a brace of hill hares caught in fine style, amidst splendid views on a crystal clear, ice-cold afternoon.

*Leading hounds from a meet of the Norfolk and Suffolk are Mr Henry Bothway MFH and Ralph Bane, his kennel huntsman.*

# *The Norfolk and Suffolk*

The Norfolk and Suffolk Foxhounds? 'There's no such pack! I can hear some of you exclaiming – but there was, albeit only from 1964 until 1968. This makes a very good hunting quiz question: which kennel-huntsman looked after a pack of staghounds, foxhounds and then harriers under the same roof, in the space of five years? The answer is Ralph Bane, Brocklesby-trained, who had the Norwich Staghounds, the Norfolk and Suffolk Foxhounds and finally the Dunston Harriers in his kennels at Wacton near Norwich. Hunting the carted deer was tremendously popular in Norfolk from the eighteenth century on, and probably before, and twenty-mile points were by no means unknown. In their closing years, from 1952 to 1964 the staghounds were hunted by that jovial, larger-than-life character, Henry Bothway. On switching to foxhounds he became a joint master and huntsman, along with Brig Harris and Charles Fellowes, and soon showed how well he had adapted to the change of quarry. Sadly, this part of Norfolk and Suffolk has no foxhunting background (the West Norfolk being some distance away). Shooting has always been a major sport in East Anglia and it was rumoured that gamekeepers were breeding a particularly fierce strain of fox-eating pheasant – which may explain their shortage when hounds drew coverts on their shoots! After four seasons it was decided to call it a day and Robert Bothway (son of Henry) and Miles Stimpson, who had been honorary secretary to the staghounds, became the first masters of the revived Dunston Harriers, which had themselves been disbanded in 1965. However, to maintain their link with the staghounds and foxhounds, it was decided that the masters and hunt staff should wear red coats instead of the green more normally associated with harriers.

*Miss Vanessa Lloyd-Davies of The Oxford University Draghunt clearing an unusual obstacle in the Heythrop country. She is now a Surgeon Captain – the first female regimental medical officer in the Household Cavalry (press photo).*

# The Oxford University Draghunt

The Oxford University Draghunt, formed in 1840, and its friendly rival at Cambridge give undergraduates the opportunity to let off steam and is a grand way of relaxing after a week of lectures. On occasions, 'letting off steam' is probably too mild an expression, especially on days of a joint meet, when the riding becomes very competitive and many a coat is muddied! Over the years many masters of the 'Oxford Drag' have gone on to greater equestrian things and include Gay Kindersley (trainer), James Teacher (Quorn), Michael Connell (Grafton), Brough Scott (television racing commentator), Marek Kwiatkowski (Meynell), Clive Preston (Bicester) and the Hon Kieron Guinness (Westmeath).

A varied country is hunted by permission of the Bicester, Grafton, Heythrop and Whaddon Chase foxhunts, with hounds being kennelled with the Bicester. Jumping is the name of the game and although it lacks the glorious uncertainty of foxhunting, it suits those short of time and the trail-layers choose the best ground and most suitable fences, unlike the jump pictured here! This was a feature of a day in the Heythrop country when the drag were entertained by that fearless cross-country rider Alan Bosley. Having dispensed ample jumping powder to the foot followers and the thirty or so riders, Alan organised several exciting lines which were jumped behind the excellent field master and joint master Miss Vanessa Lloyd-Davies, who showed the way over a line of tractors in fine style.

A child watching a drag hunt for the first time (*not* the Oxford) asked his father why the hounds weren't making much noise and was told that they were saving their breath to avoid being galloped over by the horses!

*The Cotswold Grocer '86 after winning the doghound championship at Peterborough in the show's centenary year.*

## *Peterborough Royal Foxhound Show*

'See you at Peterborough' is an often-heard remark for this show is the mecca of all foxhound breeders and a pilgrimage to be made every July. 1988 was the one hundredth show and I'm proud to say that I've only missed one since the 1939–45 War. Entries were enormous and the standard higher than ever, so it was quite amazing that all the open classes were won by just two packs, the Cotswold and the Exmoor. In 1987 the Cotswold had won their first-ever Peterborough championship with Grappler '85 and they continued in winning vein with Grocer '86. This gave enormous pleasure to their breeder, Mr Tim Unwin, who has been joint master and huntsman since 1971, and his outstandingly efficient and loyal kennel huntsman Roland Sheppard. They both appear in this picture, taken after the presentation, which also features the judges, Captain Charles Barclay MFH and Mr David Herring MFH, whilst whipper-in Richard Tabberer holds the lead.

Other packs which won classes in the centenary year were Mr Michael Poland's long-travelling Isle of Wight, the Blackmore and Sparkford Vale, the North Herefordshire and the Burton. Reserve doghound champion was South Shropshire Crockett '87, who went one better the following year, winning the top award for huntsman Michael Rowson with joint master Mr Lindsay Wallace, brother of the Exmoor's legendary Captain, carrying off the Championship Cup to be filled with champagne.

M. Jean Bocquillon with his
black-and-white buckhounds on
a bitterly cold day in the forest of
Compiègne.

The famous black-and-white
hounds in full cry.

# The Pic'ardie Valois Buckhounds

M Jean Bocquillon founded the Pic'ardie Valois buckhounds in 1956 with his brother Pierre, who left in 1968 to start his own hunt, the Forest of Troncais. M. Bocquillon is well supported by his English wife, the former Christine Dickinson, who used to hunt and point-to-point in East Anglia. This most impressive pack of large black-and-white hounds are kennelled at their home in Baron under the professional care of Robert Moreau.

For years I had heard about these famous French 'Blanc et Noire' hounds and at last, in December 1981, the opportunity arose for me to see them in action. First, however, I had to fulfil the pleasant duty of signing copies of a foxhunting book I had illustrated in a fine art gallery in Paris, sustained by champagne and caviar. Next morning, despite some six inches of snow and ten degrees of frost, I was driven to the meet of the Pic'ardie Valois Buckhounds, in the Princess section of the 30,000 acre Forest of Compiègne where I met the master M. Bocquillon.

The weather had made conditions so bad that it was dangerous, but hunt they did, although the piercing north wind increased the chill factor to a most uncomfortably low temperature. To the accompaniment of a musical fanfare, hounds were taken to draw and soon a buck was afoot. With a great cry the pack were into their stride, on a very moderate scent. The forest is intersected by well-kept rides which spread from central posts like the spokes of a wheel, so in normal conditions the field are able to gallop on excellent old turf. After a couple of hours of hunting, I climbed a steep slippery hill with M. Guy Reusse and we came upon the tracks of the hunted buck. As hounds had checked he blew the appropriate call on his horn and the pack were soon back on the line. More snow fell and it became even colder and more scentless so 'home' was blown after a melodious hunt of just three hours in the Christmas-card conditions you see in this photograph.

*Meynell.*

*Oakley.*

# The Pony Club

The Pony Club, started in the 1930s, is a marvellous institution and I'm proud to say that I was amongst its earliest members, joining the Enfield Chace branch in 1937. Many are the happy memories I have of Pony Club camps, gymkhanas and foxhunting, and I still have one small silver cup, a couple of rosettes and lots of pictures to remind me of my childhood riding experiences. In those days there were no Prince Phillip Cup games but we were still fiercely competitive, a trait which was encouraged by our instructors. I think it is terribly sad that, today, some education committees have banned competitive games on the grounds that it's bad for those who don't win – although I gather the trend is now being reversed.

Apart from the events in the summer – and Pony Club camps often provide children with their first opportunity to go away without their parents' – winter gives members the chance to go hunting. During the school holidays, special Pony Club meets are arranged when the young riders have hunting explained to them and they take turns at riding with the huntsman, whipper-in or field master, with just a few other adults on hand in case of difficulties. These special days are great fun and it is quite astonishing that many of them produce a hunt as good as any enjoyed during the whole season. The pictures here show two totally different types of country and two very different aspects of hunting. The top one shows members of the Meynell Pony Club on steaming ponies watching hounds as they check after a fast hunt whilst the lower one shows Mr Richard Bowers leading Oakley members in single file around a field of winter corn.

*HRH The Prince of Wales and Captain Ronnie Wallace MFH judging the Quorn young entry, shown by huntsman Michael Farrin.*

*Huntsmen of Welsh packs surrounding the champion Welsh foxhound, Brecon 'Greta '86', held by Johnnie Richardson from the Blencathra at the Welsh Hound Show.*

# The Puppy Show

One of the main events in any hunt's calendar is the puppy show, when the young entry are judged on conformation and ability to move. Some shows are quite small, others are enormous, yet each involves much work at the kennels, where for weeks the paintbrush has been in action and the grass lawns cut and rolled. At some, especially in Wales, each puppy walker exhibits his charge himself, kneeling down with one hand under a whiskery chin whilst the other holds aloft a feathery stern. Hounds have to be given practice at showing and this is where much patience and pounds of biscuits come into play! Hounds' names also have to be learned and it sometimes amazes me how a huntsman can pick out each hound separately from amongst perhaps ten couple of all-white ones looking as similar as peas in a pod!

The Quorn's puppy show at the Barrow-on-Soar kennels in July 1988 will go down in the hunt's history, not only because Captain Ronnie Wallace MFH was judging for the twenty-fifth year but because his co-judge was none other than HRH The Prince of Wales. Huntsman Michael Farrin, his wife Diana and all the staff scarcely slept a wink the night before but, on the day, all was well. Grandstands had been erected round the ring to provide seats for the 600 farmers and their wives who were privileged to attend whilst puppy walkers were greatly honoured to receive their puppy walkers' spoons from the Prince himself who chatted at length to each and every one.

Hounds passing Coltesbrooke church after a misty cub-hunting meet.

The front rank of the field breaking a rail during a hunt from Coltesbrooke Hall.

# The Pytchley, Northamptonshire

erhaps I am biased, but I feel that this picture of the Pytchley hounds passing Cottesbrooke Church captures all the atmosphere of early-morning autumn hunting. It was barely light enough to take the picture and the mist was still enveloping the riders behind hounds, whilst the horses' breath shows how chilly the air was. Amazingly, there was a mounted field of around 110, for this was a special meet held to celebrate the silver wedding anniversary of Peter Jones, huntsman since 1971, and his wife Monica. I can guarantee that my head wasn't the only one still throbbing at the 7 a.m. meet, after the marvellous party which had ended only a few short hours earlier.

There is no mistaking the Pytchley, formed in 1750, with their coats of Padua red, topped by a white collar. Although the country is no longer a sea of strongly fenced grass they still have lots of fun, thanks to the provision of wide, solid jumping places in each fence. However, there was not too much jumping on this morning in September 1986 as the ground was firm, whilst an overnight white frost hadn't helped. Still it was great to be out at first light to savour the sights, sounds and smells of the dawning of yet another day in this beautiful, beloved English countryside. Several foxes were hunted and a brace accounted for and I'm certain that Peter Jones will remember this special morning, no matter how many more years he hunts the Pytchley hounds.

*The Quorn bitch pack, with their huntsman Michael Farrin, moving off from a meet at Manor Farm House, Upper Broughton.*

*The front rank of the field at the start of a hunt. Dr Tom Conner rises to the fence.*

# *The Quorn,*
# *Leicestershire*

Notice how keen the Quorn hounds are in this picture – and why not for they were just completing a brilliant season, which huntsman Michael Farrin considered his best in twenty years. This was a special 'extra day' when the proceeds were donated to the Hunt Servants Benefit Society, whose governor, HRH The Prince of Wales, was on hand to receive a very substantial cheque. The meet in March 1987 was at Mr and Mrs John Copley's Manor Farm at Upper Broughton on a day which was dull and damp but – most importantly – good scenting. It was one of my better days for being in the right place at the right time and I ended up with a splendid set of pictures of the action and of the moment when hounds caught a fox.

The first draw produced a brace of foxes and the select field of seventy were soon in action as hounds raced away. Michael Farrin – surely as good a huntsman as the Quorn have ever had since their formation in 1698 – cleverly lifted hounds round a large flock of sheep and laid them on the line. On they ran almost to Old Dalby Camp and thence to Nether Broughton where, after twisting and turning around the village and the cricket field, this fox was caught in the open – a four-mile point in thirty-five minutes and many empty saddles. Then a fox on the Standard gave a fast hunt across the Clawson Lane, through Hickling village and Hickling Pastures, and a race down the vale where they were stopped. The last hunt was from Dr Tom Connor's straw bales with a fox which ran a big circle over the Muxlow grass before going to ground on the Green Lane, where 'home' was blown and the season ended.

*The hunt on the move across Romney Marsh, reflected in a big dyke.*

*A successful conclusion.*

# The Romney Marsh, Kent

What a unique and at times eerie place to hunt the Romney Marsh is. Where else can you have a day's hunting below sea level, where even a molehill takes on the appearance of a mountain in that flat, fertile and almost featureless area of mists and water and ghostly stories!

The Romney Marsh was formed in 1858. Initially the hunt staff wore the green coats of harriers despite hunting either foxes or hares, but since 1939 they have concentrated their attention on the quarry with the long brush. One of the Marsh's most notable characters – and there have been many – is Mr Alex Piper, master and huntsman from 1947 until 1966, with his whipper-in wife as joint master from 1959. In 1967 the hunt amalgamated with the East Sussex Foxhounds and the new pack has gone from strength to strength in a large and varied country along the south coast. It was during the mastership of Mr Derek Howard and Mrs Hugh Jackson that I had some really splendid days on the Marsh itself. One was from Camber, where I took colourful pictures of hounds on the beach with a wintery sea in the background, and the other from Old Romney, a few miles further inland. These flat lands are a joy for the foot follower, although some of the old turf has given way to corn and the reed-lined dykes take a deal of crossing.

Godfrey Berry, the huntsman, was trained at the Cheshire and Worcestershire and he was aided by Messers Clem and James Ramus as amateur whippers-in – members of yet another old 'Marsh' family who hunt regularly in Kent and Sussex.

Hounds were in sight all the time as there is little cover and on the occasion this picture was taken, in January 1980, hounds caught two brace of foxes (despite having to negotiate much electrified sheep-netting). I was tired, wet and muddy when Godfrey collected hounds to hack home, but filled with satisfaction at having kept up with the action all day long!

*A hat is raised in the air and huntsman Michael Jackson soon has hounds back on the line again.*

# *The Sandhurst Beagles, Berkshire*

This military pack of beagles, based at the Royal Military Academy, Sandhurst, was formed in 1935 and, despite numerous changes of masters, much-needed continuity has been provided by their stalwart professional kennel huntsmen, just three of them in all that time: Jack Cox (1935–61), Francis Moore (1961–64) and since that date Michael Jackson, who is still going as well as ever and breeding a very good-looking, level pack which also perform with great style in the field.

How well I remember this day in January 1986 with the Sandhurst! Not only because of the brilliant hunt which the beagles put on in the afternoon, but because I was soaked through twice in one day: once in the morning with the Garth and South Berks hunting around Bucklebury in pouring rain and again, after a quick change, with the beagles from their meet at the Old Elm Tree, Beech Hill, when a strong wind made the rain even more penetrating. After quickly catching a hare on rain-sodden winter corn a stronger relation was found which tested the staying powers of us foot-followers – if not the hounds – to the full. Despite the wind and rain the pack hunted most accurately and stuck to their quarry although fresh hares were disturbed on several occasions. At times hounds were obscured by spray, so wet was the ground and three times this game hare swam a swollen brook. Michael Jackson had to cast his pack a few times but they were not to be denied and after almost two hours of continuous hunting it was 'WHOOO-WHOOP!' and an exhausted crowd of followers were delighted to rest their weary legs!

*Mr Thady Ryan, master of The Scarteen 1946–86, with his famous black-and-tan hounds in unusually rocky country . . .*

*. . . and clearing a big bank and ditch.*

# The Scarteen (Black and Tans), Ireland

Over the past thirty years I've enjoyed some tremendous days with the Scarteen hounds; in fact, I've never had a bad one with those exciting black-and-tan Kerry beagles. Perhaps it's because they were the first pack I photographed in Ireland that I have a soft spot for them, but for me there has always been something magical about the atmosphere surrounding the 'Tans'. When those unique hounds start to run, their cry sends shivers down the spine. For over three centuries the Ryans of Scarteen have hunted these hounds and even through some desperately hard times they managed to continue hunting, for the love of the chase is in every Irishman's blood. Apart from the mastership – and Thady Ryan was master or joint-master and huntsman from 1946 until 1986 and is still an honorary master, although living in New Zealand – other officials are also long-serving: Percy Harris has been honorary secretary since 1936 and his 'new helper' Mrs Gwendaline Pearson, Thady Ryan's sister, joined him in 1967, whilst Tom O'Dwyer has been in charge of the kennels since 1952. 'Young' Christopher Ryan is following in his father's footsteps and has been joint master and huntsman since 1986, showing excellent sport.

However I shall never forget my first day with the 'Tans' when they met at Derk House after several nights of hard frost. 'Of course they won't hunt,' they said. They did! Of course they won't jump anything as it's far too dangerous, I thought. They did, and in no uncertain manner, with Pat Hogan leading the field in his own inimitable style, while amongst the followers were such noted horsemen as Fred Winter, Martin Molony, Greville Starkey, Lord Oaksey and Alan Lillingstone! The last time I saw Thady hunt hounds was in 1981, from Mooresfort, home of hunt chairman Arthur Moore, and again it was a red-letter day. Away from the home converts at once, it was obvious there was one 'hell' of a scent so there seemed an air of desperation about the thrusters as they tried to keep the flying pack in view and many of them failed. Meanwhile, at the front, Thady sailed on effortlessly as he had done since 1946, making it all look so easy.

# *The Shropshire Beagles*

The meet was down on the fixture card as The Sun Inn, Clun at mid-day in October 1986. However, although we partook of warming liquids at this hostelry, hounds were not unboxed until we had driven some three miles out of the village into the middle of nowhere! Soon, joint master and huntsman of the pack, formed in 1935, William Shuttleworth, pictured here, was leading his eighteen-and-a-half couple of light-framed beagles up a steeply sloping track to the high ground on Llansain Hill. On the exposed tops the westerly wind was blowing at storm force, along with icy rain squalls which lashed any uncovered area of skin like jet-propelled hailstones. Luckily, hounds soon found, in a somewhat sheltered gully and raced away into the teeth of the gale, crossing the 1400-foot contour and Offa's Dyke (*not* being walked by tourists in this foul weather). Although scent was surprisingly good, we foot-sloggers could only make slow progress and I had time to take one fascinating picture of the senior joint master Colonel David Tildesley leaning on the wind at 45 degrees actually on Offa's Dyke! Gradually we regained contact with the pack, which continued to hunt well although sometimes scent was many yards downwind of where the hare had run. Up and down the steep bracken-covered slopes those little hounds ran, their joyous voices out of all proportion to their size and number. It was a very tired but happy field which returned to their cars at the end of an exhausting yet exhilarating day on the Welsh marches.

*Mr William Shuttleworth MH leading hounds near Offa's Dyke.*

127

*The South Shropshire's huntsman heading the pack on a kennel bicycle.*

# Summer Exercise with the South Shropshire

'On your bikes then,' said South Shropshire huntsman Michael Rowson with a smile and we were away, out through the kennel gates for ninety minutes of hound exercise. It was cold at ten minutes to seven in the morning and the hounds' breath appeared as ghostly clouds of mist in the chill, still morning air. But soon we were warmed up, for the hills were steep; my bike took a strong hold but I survived without a fall, although I had not ridden one for at least thirty-five years. What a splendid sight the colourful pack made, every stern held high. Suddenly a hound spoke and it was only smart work by the whippers-in which prevented a hunt as hounds picked up a drag on the wide grass verge, probably where a fox had been foraging during the night. Finally we arrived on top of the world, or so it seemed as we halted on Lyth Hill and admired the views across the Shropshire plain and eastwards to the lofty prominence of The Wrekin.

As hounds picked at the grass, still coated with dew, and romped around like naughty schoolchildren on an outing, Michael told me something of the South Shropshire, formed in 1898, where he has been since 1968. During that time he has served under no fewer than nineteen different masters – including that rarity, a lady master who hunted hounds, Mrs Pam Wallace, who learned her trade as a whipper-in to Tom Watchorn at the Essex. During the past eight years Michael has won eleven championships at the major shows, including the tri-colour at Peterborough in 1989 with Crockett '87. They also hunt well, as a marathon day recorded on 6 January 1990 shows, when they scored a ten mile point and double that distance as hounds ran, leaving the mounted field floundering a long way behind.

*'Can you hear anything?'*

*Greg Mousley carries the terrier
for the Meynell in a satchel.*

# Terrier Men

One aspect of hunting which never ceases to amaze me is that, no matter how long and fast hounds run and no matter how inaccessible the place, within minutes of marking to ground, the terrier man is on the spot. On occasions in steep and rugged country, I have been first to the earth but usually the tireless terrier man is there before me, ready to bolt the fox. In bygone days, the whipper-in often carried a terrier in a satchel but today I only know of one hunt where this still happens – at the Meynell where Greg Mousley wears a red coat and carries his terrier in a bag on his lap, jumping those big fences as they come. Nowadays most hunts provide their terrier men with a Land Rover so they are able to traverse muddy lanes without fear of getting stuck (although why more of them don't turn over on steep hillsides I'll never know).

The other part of the terrier man's work involves long hours and a fantastic knowledge of the hunt's country. I refer of course to the very necessary task of earth-stopping. Very few people realise what a great difference to their sport a top class earth-stopper can make. It means tramping about the countryside either at night or in the very early morning, inspecting all known holes, and I've often witnessed how irate a huntsman can become if a fox goes to ground in a place which should have been stopped. The majority of terrier men remain incognito, but a few are known outside their own countries: Charles Parker, David Allibone, Cyril Smith and Roger Bigland, to name but a few, are terrier men of long standing who have earned their fame the hard way.

*Hunting on foot with the indomitable United, after heavy overnight snow and frost.*

# *The United,*
# *Welsh Borders*

'Yes we'll be hunting as usual, with the meet at Acton Cross Roads, but it'll be a day on foot as there's six to nine inches of snow!' This was huntsman Rodney Ellis's reply to my telephone query. Of course I'd guessed they would be hunting as it takes more than a spot of snow to stop those hardy farmers of the United Hunt, formed in 1837, whose superb hill and grass country straddles the Shopshire/Montgomery borders. Back in the mid 1960s, I had some grand days with Rodney when he whipped-in to Charlie Appleyard at the Morpeth. Later he saw service at the West Norfolk, Tiverton and Old Berkshire before coming to the United where he met and married Georgiana Hardy – they are now joint masters of the hunt.

This morning in January 1987 dawned bright but bitterly cold, with 10 degrees of frost and fresh snow on the hills which had drifted in places to a depth of four feet. This caused a few dramas for some of the shorter members of the field. However, there was a scent and those English and Welsh cross-hounds bustled their fox round the first covert before racing away through flocks of sheep, with us followers floundering behind. Down into the valley they ran, checking by the stream, then on uphill again to some old farm buildings where it is probable our quarry found a hole. By now the twenty or so energetic followers were rosy-faced and steaming with the exertion of running through snowdrifts. A couple of further hunts took place, with one fox being added to the tally, before Rodney blew for home to end a day snatched from the jaws of an icy winter.

*Retiring huntsman Jim Bennett leading hounds from his farewell meet of The Vale of Aylesbury, in 1987.*

*Hounds after catching a fox.*

## The Vale of Aylesbury, Herts, Bucks, Beds, Oxon

There are always long faces amongst the hunting fraternity when the words 'to finish the season' appear on the fixture card. Sometimes an aura of sadness can be felt in the air when a retirement is imminent, and this was very much the case for the Vale of Aylesbury Hunt on Saturday 21 March 1987 when their much-loved huntsman, Jim Bennett, came to his farewell meet.

I first met Jim in 1952 when he was whipper-in to Nimrod Champion at the Ledbury. The following season he moved to the Old Berkeley as kennel-huntsman and then as huntsman in 1955. The Vale of Aylesbury Hunt was formed in 1970, with the amalgmation of the Hertfordshire, South Oxfordshire and Old Berkeley countries, with the new pack appointing Jim as huntsman and retaining the yellow livery which goes back to the eighteenth century and the Earls of Berkeley. Despite the inevitable problems brought about by every amalgamation, Jim continued to show splendid sport throughout the enormous new country which measures some forty miles from north to south and a similar distance from east to west.

The farewell meet was at Rossway, home of the Hadden-Paton family, and long before the appointed hour of mid-day, the park was full of horses and foot followers. Former masters, numerous hunt staff and friends swelled the mounted field to 150, all intent on enjoying 'Jim's last day'. After the speeches and good wishes for his retirement in Dorset, Jim led hounds away to draw for the last time, with a colourful cavalcade close behind. The first fox was found near to where I was standing and I viewed him across the ride. For twenty minutes hounds raced round this covert before it was 'WHOO-WHOOP' right at my feet. Another fox was found and quickly left covert with hounds hot on his brush. The mounted field had plenty of jumping, for this part of the country is well fenced and there were several muddy coats as the pace began to tell. After a fast hunt through woods and fields, hounds marked to ground after a five-mile run with a four-mile point and Jim's smile was even broader than usual.

*Mr James Crosbie Dawson MFH, taking the Vine and Craven hounds across the river Kennet, to hunt a small island.*

## The Vine and Craven, Berkshire, Hampshire and Wiltshire

Two long-established packs of foxhounds, the Craven founded in 1739 and the Vine some thirty years later, combined in 1968 to form one very large country under the mastership of Mr Michael Renny. Although somewhat reduced over the years by urban expansion and new roads, their country extends through the counties of Berkshire, Hampshire and Wiltshire, which are all noted for high-class pheasant shoots. However, relations between the two sports are good and it has been proved time and time again that with good keeping, foxes and pheasants can and do survive together.

This picture was taken in November 1980 during the mastership of Mrs Sandra Edwards, Messrs Robin Mackenzie, Dermot Magill and James Crosbie Dawson, who carried the horn. Hounds had met on a dull November morning, with a bitterly cold east wind numbing the senses, at Shalford Bridge, Wasing. The Rod Beds close to the A4 road, the Kennett and Avon Canal and the main railway provided the first fox which ran to the sewage beds where scent proved catchy! Held on, the pack ran slowly through several strips of woodland before being stopped by the village. Now came the chance to take the picture shown here as James Crosbie Dawson led hounds over a rickety bridge across the River Kennet onto an island which held a brace of foxes. After they had been dealt with, the rest of the day was spent in and around the 350 acres of Wasing Wood, with its well-kept rides and its population of foxes, pheasants and roe deer, all of which were viewed by the hunt followers.

*Godfrey Berry,* top, *huntsman of the East Sussex and Romney Marsh, and Captain Ian Farquhar,* left, *master of the Duke of Beaufort's Hunt, showing how to jump wire.*

# Ware Wire!

In the 1990s there are not many hunts where during a day's sport the cry of 'Ware wire!' is not heard at least once. Over the past forty-two years, during which I have photographed hounds all over the world, there has been a tremendous increase in the amount of wire to be found in the countryside. This is bad enough when it's visible, but when it is hidden in the top few inches of a thorn hedge it can be a killer. So often, modern hedges are machine-trimmed and invariably have wire on each side, making a double oxer, whereas in less mechanised times hedges were cut and laid by hand. In these cases the bottoms were so thick that wire was unnecessary but with a solid binder at the top horses still had to jump cleanly or a fall was the likely result. Looking at many hunting countries, especially in Wales where there is a tremendous amount of grass, one's first impression is that the hedges are clean, but a closer inspection reveals a veritable tangle of wire in each fence, as those active Welsh sheep are so difficult to keep in. A recent addition to the hazards are electric fences which are not only hard to see, but give hounds a nasty shock which can put them off for the rest of the day as they can't understand what is happening.

People hunting in Ireland have always seemed to jump wire and now they are doing the same over here. This is fine if you trust your horse and are certain that he has seen it before being asked to jump. On occasions I've seen a sack, or even a coat, placed on the top strand of a wire fence to give an eye-line; others I know walk up to the fence and tap it, so that the horse can see it and knows it's there; either way, wire is a dangerous but ever-more frequent obstacle out hunting.

*The Westerby Hunt crossing frozen turf at Naseby, where the great battle took place in 1645.*

*Hounds crossing a bridge during a bitterly cold day at Naseby.*

# The Westerby Basset Hounds, Northamptonshire

Formed in the nineteenth century and known variously as the Slane Bassets and the Walhampton, the Westerby hunt over the Fernie, Atherstone and Pytchley countries, and their hounds – now labelled English Bassets – owe their origin to Lt Col Eric Morrison who was a joint master and huntsman from 1932 to 1939 and between 1947 and 1951. However, since 1956 the Bevin family have been in charge: Charles Bevin was master and huntsman from 1956 until 1981 and his son William has carried on his father's good work since 1983 with equal success.

In 1645 the Battle of Naseby was fought between the Roundheads and the Cavaliers and on the day of my visit to Naseby in February 1978 we had to fight another battle – though happily of a less bloody nature. This time it was a contest between the ferocious wintery weather, which had held Britain in its grasp for too long, and the Westerby Bassets. I'm happy to say that the latter won by a convincing knockout! The meet on that bitterly cold day in February was at Mill Hill, and a crowd of around a hundred, including grounded foxhunters, were in attendance, to watch fourteen couple of bassets show their low-scenting ability on the frozen ground. And show it they did. Dragging up to their first hare across ankle-breaking plough, on which they puzzled out the line with great patience, it was a welcome change for us foot-sloggers and no doubt for the hounds too, when we moved on to old turf, hard though it was. At first we ran all round Naseby Fields, where the actual battle took place, skirting sheep, before getting into top gear and racing towards Sulby, with a grand cry. Crossing the Welford road they checked by the icy brook but a good cast round more sheep had them going again. By now it was even colder, yet when hounds were eventually stopped amongst fresh hares by the Portly-Ford gravel pits, there were still thirty hardy followers in close attendance.

*Long-serving kennel-huntsman Jim Bunch leading hounds to a very wet meet of the Western at the Ding Dong mine.*

*The field crossing rough country in pouring rain.*

# The Western, Cornwall

The Western Hunt was founded around 1820 and encompasses the western end of Cornwall, including Land's End and numerous craggy cliffs for it is bounded on three sides by the sea. Inland there are areas of cultivation for market gardening well suited to the temperate climate and comparative freedom from hard frosts. There are many parts which are rugged, wild and hilly where bracken, gorse and brambles thrive as do rhododendrons – so there is plenty of covert for foxes to shelter in.

It has been known to rain on the Cornish Moors and it certainly didn't disappoint us on my day out with the Western in January 1966. Captain Ben Sparrow, master or joint master and huntsman 1950–76, had invited me to stay at his picturesque home near to the quaintly named village of Mousehole and I remember well sitting down to dine on that local delicacy woodcock for the first time in my life. My visit was not only to see the Western hounds in action, but also to witness the race from the Ding Dong Mine, a cross-country race over a natural line of hunting country (as were the original point-to-points). Conditions were appalling, with torrential rain driven by a strong wind and low cloud at times blocking out the beautiful countryside. However, those hardy Cornish hunting folk were not deterred and set off in a bunch at a rousing gallop over the moors, slowing slightly at each imposing wall or bank, with Tim le Grice running out a convincing winner. Then hounds arrived under the care of their famous kennel huntsman Jim Bunch who was in charge for a record forty-eight years, from 1938–86. A busy day's hunting ensued over rugged country and the occasional grazing meadows, with hounds doing well in conditions which did not encourage foxes to travel far from their home coverts.

*Huntsman Terry Richmond blowing 'home' at the end of a good day's hunting with The West Somerset Vale.*

# *The West Somerset Vale,*
# *Somerset*

I
t is often the case that when a long mastership finishes the hunt concerned goes through a traumatic time until things settle down again. This was certainly what happened to the West Somerset Vale, formed in 1946, when the twenty-one-year joint mastership of Messers Ayre and Chidgey, who had shown such excellent sport throughout, came to an end in 1985. Three times in three seasons thereafter control of the hunt changed hands but now things seem to have come good, with Mrs Hillary Roe settled in as sole master and the very experienced Terry Richmond as huntsman. Mrs Roe's late father-in-law was master from 1951 until 1961 so it is appropriate that she now lives in his old home at Swang, near Bridgewater. Terry Richmond, former huntsman to the Wheatland, where he produced many top-class show hounds, brought a couple of good brood bitches from there, and from the Cheshire, to form the nucleus of a new breeding policy. Proving just how well things have worked out for them, Caliph '89 won the dog hound championship at Builth Wells, the first in the hunt's history to carry this off.

The country is quite small and hilly, with plenty of grass, some woods and some arable, including root crops, which give good cover to the useful population of foxes. As happens so often in hunting country nowadays, there is wire, both barbed and electric, the latter being a particular problem as it soon upsets hounds.

For my visit in December 1987, hounds met at Charlynch, and it was good to see Terry Chidgey, who carried the horn from 1977 to 1985 helping the Hon Gill Spens and John West with the whipping-in, whilst the master, immaculate as ever, was in charge of the large mounted field. A blue haze did nothing for the scenting conditions, but the pack stuck to their task and accounted for a brace of foxes – the second one, after running through a pheasant wood, encouraged by Donald Hooper the gamekeeper. The day ended with horses being washed off in the duck pond at Swang, before we retired inside to discuss the day's sport over an enormous and much-needed hunting tea.

*Mrs Elsie Morgan MFH with her hounds, which were bred with such success on Mr Ikey Bell's lines for The West Waterford.*

*The Master jumping a bank with wire.*

# The West Waterford, Ireland

In 1953 the fortunes of the West Waterford Hunt were at a low ebb. Major and Mrs Anthony Burke had just given up the mastership and no immediate successor was in sight, so, just to help out for a little while, Mrs Elsie Morgan took over as master and huntsman, with her husband Captain Tom Morgan as whipper-in. Happily, Elsie proved to be a natural at the job and soon Tom joined her in a mastership which was to last until 1984 – somewhat more than 'a little while'! With hounds kennelled at their Bishopstown home, they embarked on a breeding policy which was to revolutionise the pack and make it unique in Ireland. Seeking advice from one of this century's greatest exponents of hound breeding, Mr Ikey Bell MFH (master of the Blazers 1903–08, the Kilkenny 1908–21 and the South and West Wilts 1925–34), they imported much fell-hound blood, mostly from Sir Alfred Goodson's College Valley, which resulted in a pack of mainly white hounds. When I first saw them being hunted by Elsie in 1964, it was a revelation: they were fast, hunted accurately and with tremendous cry and were great fox-catchers – some achievement in that wild country, with its moorland, pasture, bogs, banks and stonewalls. It was hard on the followers as well! On that first day there was a broken leg and one broken arm whilst I spent the evening removing gorse prickles from various parts of my anatomy.

My last visit to Tom and Elsie came in January 1983 when there was a celebration meet at Clashmore to mark Elsie's seventieth birthday. Age did not seem to have affected her and, although she had given up top-class show jumping, she and Tom were still producing top-quality show horses and hunters, many for export. The day's sport was as good as ever – Elsie by her hounds' side when they needed help, Tom in charge of the field and both of them jumping banks and wire like twenty-year-olds; we shall not see their like again.

*Mr Dorian Williams MFH and
his huntsman Albert Buckle at
the end of their twenty-sixth and
last season in office, at The
Whaddon Chace.*

*Dorian Williams in action.*

## The Whaddon Chase, Buckinghamshire

I first met Dorian Williams in 1952, during his mastership of the Grafton, and in that same year I stayed at the North Cotswold Hunt kennels in Broadway with Albert Buckle. Little did I then realise that they would combine their talents at the Whaddon Chase, to form a most famous partnership lasting from 1954 until 1980. Dorian Williams, an immensely popular writer, speaker and commentator, was a marvellous ambassador for foxhunting during his long mastership, spreading the word about field sports far and wide. As huntsman Albert Buckle was not only good at his job but he and his wife Kath became pillars of strength to the Whaddon Chase followers. I think that I had a day with them during each of those twenty-six brilliant seasons, so it was a sad occasion for me as well as for all their friends when finally, in March 1980, Dorian had his last day as master and Albert his last as huntsman. The weather had been terribly wet and the land was sodden, but the local farmers never considered calling it off so a tremendous crowd gathered at Stoke Road Farm, Stewkley, home of those great supporters the Stone family. Despite being in pain from a bone-breaking fall a few days earlier, Dorian rode to the meet on his grey hunter although he was unable to follow hounds across country. His joint master since 1969, Peter Stoddart, took over as field master but sadly he too had a crashing fall during the first hunt and had to 'retire hurt', thus missing the remainder of an excellent if muddy outing. Albert, crossing the strongly fenced country as well on his last day as his first in 1954, had hounds in top gear and many memories were stirred when those famous coverts High Haven and Christmas Gorse were drawn. By a coincidence, the last fox ran to the Quainton Hills and hounds were stopped at George Simms's Farm, where a spirited party was soon under way – both masters attending, as you see here, with their damaged arms in slings and attired in sports jackets and slacks!

# Ystrad Hunt

When I was invited to visit the Ystrad Hunt in the Rhondda Valley, little did I imagine that the meet would be at a Conservative Club for I didn't think there was one in this Labour Party stronghold! Yet there they were; 12 couple of mostly Welsh hounds in the main street at Maerdy, with their huntsman Rowley Miles and four joint masters. For those ill-informed critics who think that all masters are landed gentry I would point out that this quartet are all down-to-earth hard working men. One deals in second-hand cars; one is a butcher; one drives lorries and the senior master Mr Michael Whitby is a milkman who starts work at 3.30 am in order to finish his round in time to go hunting! A fox was found on a rough bank of white grass within 400 yards of the meet and ran uphill, through the woods to the open tops at 1500 feet. On, almost to Treorchy, famous for its male voice choir, then right handed across the slag heaps whose stark black outlines were softened by snow left from the previous week's blizzards. For 40 minutes hounds ran well before marking to ground in an old quarry. Hacking on to the next draw, Rowley Miles led the pack past the still working Maerdy colliery (illustrated here) and over the Pont Llyswen to higher ground from where the best hunt of the day began. Found above the reservoir, the fox ran to the Tyla forestry and out to the Rhigos road, crossing the steep valley onto the open mountainous moorland and into the Bwllfa Cwmdare coverts. A similar circle was then run, with hounds being stopped in dense hill fog after a fast 8 mile run amidst spectacular scenery, and we all returned to the Conservative Club for much need refreshment and a sing-song.